START

START

TERRY VIRGO

Edited by
Mary Austin

KINGSWAY PUBLICATIONS
EASTBOURNE

First published by Word Books, Nelson Word Ltd
This new edition published by Kingsway 1999

Co-published in South Africa with SCB Publishers
Cornelis Struik House, 80 McKenzie Street
Cape Town 8001, South Africa
Reg no 04/02203/06

ISBN 0 85476 831 9

Published by
KINGSWAY PUBLICATIONS
Lottbridge Drove, Eastbourne, BN23 6NT, England.
E-mail: books@kingsway.co.uk

Cover design by Pinnacle Creative

Designed and produced for the publishers by
Bookprint Creative Services, P.O. Box 827, BN21 3YJ, England.
Printed in Great Britain

Contents

Acknowledgements

This book has been designed to help Christians apply the word of God to their lives and grow in their faith. It contains thirty-one undated studies, each of which provides teaching on a relevant theme and suggests ways in which that teaching may be applied to everyday life.

The studies have been handled by different internationally renowned authors who have been specifically chosen because of their proven effectiveness in a particular area of teaching and ministry.

Our thanks go to the following for their contributions: Michael Eaton, R. T. Kendall, C. J. Mahaney, Larry Tomczak and Joseph C. Wongsak.

Making the Most of These Studies

Welcome to a new start in life. You're not here by chance. Long before you were born God decided that he wanted you here. He watched over you, even though you didn't know it, then he drew you to himself. Now he wants you to learn more about him and about how to live the life he has planned for you.

We suggest that you take about an hour, or as long as you need, to cover each study. You might want to work through the material more quickly, but if you take your time, you are likely to benefit more. The important thing is not that you finish fast, but that you hear from God en route! So aim to learn well and steadily build the teaching into your life. We recommend that you use the New International Version of the Bible.

If you are a new Christian you may have many questions. Where do I go from here? Should I be baptised? How can I get the most out of the Bible? Why is prayer important? Do I need to join a church? What about giving, the Holy Spirit and tongues? Maybe you've asked these kinds of questions. This book should answer them.

The sections under the main text relate to the teaching material. You may be asked to consider some aspect of the Christian life, to write down an answer, or to do something practical. The questions have been designed to help you understand more about Jesus and how you can live life 'to the full' (John 10:10). Let the Scripture verses inspire you in your walk with God.

The Bible says, 'Wise men store up knowledge' (Proverbs 10:14), and Jesus underlines this when he calls us to '[bring] good things out of the good stored up in [our] hearts' (Luke 6:45).

God wants to encourage and inform you through his word. That's what these studies are all about: to give you the invaluable opportunity to hear direct from God and to store up what he says to you. Please use a separate notebook for your answers. Not only will it help you to crystallise your thoughts, but it will also be of tremendous reference value in the future.

As you study, refuse to let time pressurise you. Pray that God will speak to you personally, and expect him to do so. You may sometimes find that you're so enthralled by what he says to you that you're looking up many scriptures which are not even suggested!

Finally, may God bless you as you learn, and as you live your life for him.

START

Conversion is no repairing of the old building: but it takes all down and erects a new structure. The sincere Christian is quite a new fabric, from the foundation to the root all is new.

Joseph Alleine

1

Lost and Found

We all, like sheep, have gone astray, each of us has turned to his own way; and the Lord has laid on him the iniquity of us all. (Isaiah 53:6)

You were like sheep going astray, but now you have returned to the Shepherd and Overseer of your souls. (1 Peter 2:25)

Jesus once told a story about a sheep that wandered away from the sheepfold and got lost. It would have died if its owner hadn't gone out to look for it, and to bring it back (Luke 15:3–7).

You were once like that lost sheep – roaming around, maybe trying to find answers to life's questions. Perhaps your search led you into some disasters which you'd rather not recall. Then you heard about Jesus, and the amazing sacrifice he made to bring you back to God.

You once lived independently of God, and your sinful ways separated you from him and made him angry. You may have thought that by being good you could win his favour and shake off your guilt. Then you discovered that you couldn't do anything to help yourself. You needed a Saviour – and God had provided one.

God was delighted with his Son. Everything Jesus did was perfect. He helped people, healed them and taught them the truth. But he didn't come into the world just to be a good example, as some people think. He came to 'seek and to save what was lost' (Luke 9:10).

When Jesus died on the cross, some people thought that he was suffering for his own sin. But he was suffering for ours. We deserved the punishment that he went through. We were the guilty ones; he was innocent. But he let God punish him so that we could live.

When you turned your back on sin (repented) and asked Jesus to forgive you, he immediately took away all your sin by his death on the cross. In return, he gave you all his righteousness, completely restored your broken relationship with God, and promised you eternal life.

You didn't earn this salvation, nor did you deserve it. God simply said, 'I want you,' and in faith you responded to him. You were saved by grace: the free, unmerited favour of God.

So you haven't had a little change that will make you a bit happier and more religious. Jesus, the great Shepherd, has brought you back to God. When he died, you died too, and 'your life is now hidden with Christ in God' (Colossians 3:3). You have a brand new identity.

When God looks at you, he doesn't see a sinner any more. He sees the righteousness of Jesus, and he loves you as much as he loves his Son. You've been 'born again' (John 3:3). You're a totally new creation – 'the old has gone, the new has come!' (2 Corinthians 5:17).

➔ Food for thought

Salvation is a gift.

- 'I give them eternal life, and they shall never perish; no-one can snatch them out of my hand' (John 10:28).
- 'For the wages of sin is death, but the gift of God is eternal life in Christ Jesus our Lord' (Romans 6:23).
- 'For it is by grace you have been saved, through faith – and this is not from yourselves, it is the gift of God – not by works, so that no-one can boast' (Ephesians 2:8–9).

➔ To discover

- Look up the words 'sin' and 'righteousness' in a dictionary and write down what they mean.
- Read Luke 15:3–7.
  - Who rejoiced when you became a Christian?
  - In what ways do you think you might have been like a sheep straying and needing to be found?
- Read Philippians 3:3–6:
  - Note the confidence that Paul once had in his flesh (in himself).
  - In your notebook write down the things that you could boast about (e.g. good looks, money, intelligence, abilities, manners, possessions, etc.).

● Now read Philippians 3: 7–11 and see how becoming a Christian changed Paul's thinking.

→ To consider

● Consider whether your confidence is now in yourself or in Christ.

The most exciting thing for me as a new Christian was the knowledge that God was real, that he loved me and that, unlike humans, he would never let me down. A relationship with a caring Father represented for me a permanent security – a security which I had longed for.

[Bob] Margaret Ellis

2

Life to the Full

'I have come that they may have life, and have it to the full.'
(John 10:10)

Jesus rose from the dead. What's the most obvious
meaning of the word 'resurrection'? The restoration of
life. When Jesus died, he didn't just offer you forgiveness and a place in heaven. He invited you to live! You
were spiritually dead in your sins. Jesus laid down his
life for you so that he could give his life to you – life to
the full.

Now only Jesus could live life to the full. You can't,
because you're not good enough – that's why you must
live by faith. The Bible says that you've been crucified
with Christ and your old life is dead. Dead people can't
do anything! So the only way you can have abundant
life is by letting Jesus live his life through you.

You're alive in Christ. Your life is united with his, and
what God gave to his Son when he was on earth, he
gives to you. He loves you like Jesus and tells you that
you're his child. He invites you to enjoy an intimate
relationship with him and to call him 'Father' just as

Jesus did. He wants you to pray to him and hear his voice. He longs to meet all your needs and use you powerfully to glorify his name.

The world searches high and low for life – security, love, joy, peace, purpose and hope. All these things are yours in Christ. You've committed yourself to him; he has committed himself to you. He is with you. He is working in you. He will never let you down. Maybe you've found it hard to trust people in the past. Well, here's someone you can always rely on. 'I am with you always,' he said (Matthew 28:20). And that's a promise.

Unbelievers think that enjoying life is about money, sex, power and having a good time. While Jesus doesn't want you to sin, he does invite you to have fun. But he wants you to see that real life is about knowing him (John 17:3). Receiving Jesus as your Saviour is only the first step. Now he wants you to know him – to read about him in the Bible and to discover what a great friend and King he really is.

So forget the little Sunday school pictures you get of a spineless, pathetic Jesus, and take a good look at his life. See his intimacy with God, his joy, his confidence, his faith, his power. Note how compassionately he dealt with people who needed help, and how masterfully he defeated those who opposed him. Here was a man who lived life to the full, a man who invites you by faith to do the same.

➔ Food for thought

Life is wrapped up in Jesus.

- 'I am the bread of life' (John 6:48).
- 'I am the resurrection and the life' (John 11:25).
- 'I am...the life' (John 14:6).
- 'These things are written so that you may believe that Jesus is the Christ...and that by believing you may have life in his name' (John 20:31).
- 'He who has the Son has life; he who does not have the Son of God does not have life' (1 John 5:12).

➔ To discover

- Read John 17:3. Note that 'eternal life' doesn't start in heaven, it begins now.
- Some people think that God wants to make life miserable. Read the second part of 1 Timothy 6:17. How do you know that God wants you to enjoy life?
- Look up the following verses and write down in your notebook what God will give you:
  – John 16:13;
  – Romans 15:13;
  – 2 Corinthians 1:3–4;
  – 2 Thessalonians 2:16–17;
  – 2 Thessalonians 3:3;
  – Hebrews 4:16;
  – James 1:5;
  – 1 John 1:5.

⇥ To consider

- The Christian faith is based on facts, not feelings. Sometimes you might not feel very close to Jesus. Of course, if you've done something to offend him, you'll feel guilty and must repent. But if you haven't done anything wrong, you must believe by faith that he loves you and hasn't abandoned you. You must learn to trust what the Bible says more than how you feel.
- Ask Jesus to help you do this.

The disciple of Christ cannot lose: when he gives all, he gains all; when he loses his life, he finds it.

David Watson

3

Follow Me

As Jesus was walking beside the Sea of Galilee, he saw two brothers, Simon called Peter and his brother Andrew. They were casting a net into the lake, for they were fishermen. 'Come, follow me,' Jesus said, 'and I will make you fishers of men.' At once they left their nets and followed him. (Matthew 4:18–20)

'Come, follow me.' That's what Jesus said to the people who became his first disciples. They obviously saw him as someone worth following. So they left behind their old life and joined him. From that time on, he was their leader and they were his disciples.

Jesus has called you to follow him. You've left your old life behind, and now you're his disciple. But what does discipleship mean? Let's see.

First, it involves obedience. That's not a popular word. Most people prefer to choose whether they obey or not. 'I don't want to be restricted,' they think. But Jesus won't restrict us. He loves us and proved that love by laying down his life for us. He wants us to have life 'to the full' (John 10:10), but he can't give it to us unless we obey what he says. We must trust him. Obedience leads to freedom, not bondage.

Second, it involves serving. Early on, the disciples really didn't understand what it meant to serve others. They wanted status not service, and argued over who was the greatest among them (Luke 22:24). They also fell into self-pity. Peter pointed out to Jesus what they'd had to sacrifice to follow him (Luke 18:28). God can't use us if we're seeking position or demanding certain conditions of service. Jesus stooped and washed the disciples' feet. That's the spirit of service that he calls us to imitate.

Third, it involves simplicity. Jesus laid aside all earthly security and depended on God alone. He called his disciples to follow his example (Luke 12:33). While he probably won't ask us to give everything away, he does encourage us to live simply and to rely on God to meet all our needs. That's quite a challenge in a society which tells us to get and hoard as much wealth as we can.

Fourth, it involves suffering. Jesus suffered, and warned his disciples they would suffer too. They did – physically, mentally and spiritually. If we follow Jesus, we can't avoid suffering. But often, when our suffering is greatest, God is working most deeply in our lives.

Jesus' great goal was to glorify God, not seek personal satisfaction. He isn't after half-hearted Christians who just want to have a good time. He's looking for disciples who will count the cost and get on with the tasks that he gives them. Jesus has chosen you to live for his glory. You're his disciple. Follow him.

➔ Food for thought

We've been called to serve.

- 'Whoever wants to become great among you must be your servant, and whoever wants to be first must be your slave' (Matthew 20:26–27).
- 'Whoever serves me must follow me; and where I am, my servant also will be. My Father will honour the one who serves me' (John 12:26).
- 'Each one should use whatever gift he has received to serve others' (1 Peter 4:10).

➔ To discover

- Read John 14:15, 1 John 5:3 and 2 John 1:6.
  - How do you demonstrate your love for Jesus?
  - Where do you find his 'commands'?
- Read Luke 14:25–33. (*Note*: 'Hate' in verse 25 isn't literal. Jesus is saying that our love for him must be so great that our love for others or ourselves seems like hate in comparison.) In the light of verse 33, do you really want to be Jesus' disciple?

➔ To consider

- Seriously consider what the cost of discipleship might be for you.
- In your notebook, write down anything that Jesus

challenges you about (e.g. ending a relationship; returning something you've stolen; forgiving someone who's hurt you badly; writing a letter of apology, etc.). Do whatever he tells you.

The phrase in Matthew 28:19, 'baptising them into the Name' . . . would indicate that the baptised person was closely bound to, or became the property of, the one into whose Name he was baptised.

W. E. Vine

4

Be Baptised

Christ died for our sins according to the Scriptures . . .
he was buried . . . he was raised on the third day.
(1 Corinthians 15:3–4)

Now that you're a Christian, do you have to be baptised
(plunged underwater) – even if you were christened as
a baby? Maybe you don't really want to stand up and
tell everyone what has happened to you. Maybe
baptism by immersion sounds like a crazy idea. But if
you look at what the Bible says about it, you'll see why
it's so important.

Baptism is a sign that someone's sins have been
washed away. Jesus didn't have any sin, so he is the
person you'd least expect to be baptised. So why did he
ask John the Baptist to baptise him? What was he doing
in the River Jordan surrounded by wicked people who
were all confessing their sins? He should have been
helping John to baptise sinners, not going through
baptism himself!

Jesus humbled himself and was baptised not because
he'd sinned, but because he wanted to identify with

sinners. As he stood there waiting to be baptised, he knew exactly what his baptism would symbolise. When he went down into the water and came up again, he would be acting out his death and resurrection.

The moment you became a Christian, your life was linked with Christ. You were baptised into him and what happened to him happened to you as well. You died with him to sin and to its power over you. And you rose with him to a brand new life. When Jesus was baptised, he was identifying with you. When you're baptised, you're identifying with him.

When you go down into the water, you are saying, 'Lord Jesus, you died on the cross for me. From now on, my old life is dead. I've broken with sin.' While you're under the water, you are saying, 'Lord, just as you were buried in the tomb, so my old sinful life is now buried in the water. This baptism is my funeral.' And when you're lifted out of the water, you are saying, 'Lord, you were raised from the dead by God's power, and by that power I can now live a totally new life.'

Perhaps baptism will be really costly for you, and you wonder if you can go through with it. But Jesus was baptised, and he knew that his death would cost him everything. He never asks you to do what he hasn't done before. He wants you to identify with him in baptism, to confess openly, 'I'm in Christ! The old life is dead and buried. From now on, Jesus is my Lord and I'm living only for him.'

➔ Food for thought

Christians are united in Christ's death.

- 'I have been crucified with Christ and I no longer live, but Christ lives in me. The life I live in the body, I live by faith in the Son of God' (Galatians 2:20).
- 'All of you who were baptised into Christ have clothed yourselves with Christ' (Galatians 3:27).
- '[You have] been buried with him in baptism and raised with him through your faith in the power of God, who raised him from the dead' (Colossians 2:12).

➔ To discover

- The Greek word for 'baptism' means 'dip, submerge, or cleanse by washing'. New Christians were baptised by total immersion. They were baptised in large groups, as individuals and in families. Check that this is true by looking up the following verses:
  - Acts 2:37–41;
  - Acts 8:26–34;
  - Acts 16:29–34.
- Read Matthew 28:20. Does Jesus want new Christians to be baptised?
- Read Acts 10:48. Do you think that new Christians should be baptised, even if they don't feel like it?

➔ To consider

- Read Romans 6:3–14 and write down in your notebook the answers to the following questions:
  - Who are we baptised into (v.3)?
  - What are we baptised into (v.3)?

– Which part of us has been crucified (v.6)?
– Why does it need to die (v.7)?
– How could you offer the parts of your body to sin (v.13)? Give practical examples.
– How could you offer the parts of your body to righteousness (v.13)? Give practical examples.

God means all Christians . . . to enjoy the full inward blessing of Pentecost . . . right from the moment of their conversion.

J. I. Packer

5

The Holy Spirit

As soon as Jesus was baptised, he went up out of the water. At that moment heaven was opened, and he saw the Spirit of God descending like a dove and lighting on him. (Matthew 3:16)

'It is for your good that I am going away. Unless I go away, the Counsellor will not come to you; but if I go, I will send him to you.' (John 16:7)

Immediately Jesus was baptised, the Holy Spirit came down on him. He chose not to live by his own power as the Son of God, but to rely totally on the power of the Holy Spirit. He wanted his disciples to follow his example.

The disciples saw the power of the Spirit in the life of Jesus. He preached with authority and amazed them by his miracles. So when he told them, 'It's better for you if I go away,' they must have thought, 'No way! It's better if you stay.' But if Jesus had stayed, the Spirit wouldn't have come.

Jesus knew that while he was confined to a human

body, he could only be in one place at a time. But if he returned to heaven, he could send the Spirit to his disciples. Then they could be in different places and he'd be working by his Spirit through them all.

Jesus didn't want his disciples to begin their ministry until they had received his power. So he told them to wait, and he promised that he would send them the Holy Spirit from heaven – a promise he fulfilled on the Day of Pentecost. The disciples were praying together and the Spirit came down on them (Acts 2:1–4). The experience changed them from a group of fearful people (John 20:19) to a dynamic company who won many thousands to Christ.

New Christians are all born of the Spirit (John 3:5–8), but they still need to be baptised in (filled with) the Spirit. When a man called Philip preached the gospel in Samaria, many people believed in Jesus and were baptised in water. But they weren't filled with the Spirit until a few days later (Acts 8:12–17).

Other people were converted and filled with the Spirit on the same day. The apostle Paul met a group of Jews who had been baptised by John, but who weren't Christians. He led them to Christ and baptised them. When he laid his hands on them, they were instantly filled with the Spirit (Acts 19:1–7). Cornelius and his family were even filled with the Spirit before they were baptised in water (Acts 10:34–48).

Sometimes the Spirit falls on believers when other Christians lay hands on them; sometimes he comes on them when there is no physical contact. Jesus says that the Spirit is like the wind (John 3:8). We can't pin him down and predict how he is going to move. But we can

seek the same experience of the Spirit that Jesus and his
disciples had.

➔ Food for thought

We must rely on the Spirit's power.

- 'My message and my preaching were not with wise
  and persuasive words, but with a demonstration of
  the Spirit's power, so that your faith might not rest
  on men's wisdom, but on God's power' (1
  Corinthians 2:5).
- 'We have this treasure in jars of clay to show that
  this all-surpassing power is from God and not from
  us' (2 Corinthians 4:7).
- '[God's] power is made perfect in weakness'
  (2 Corinthians 12:9).

➔ To discover

- Read the following and reflect on how people
  received the Holy Spirit:
  - Acts 2:1–4;
  - Acts 8:12–17;
  - Acts 10:34–48;
  - Acts 19:1–7.
- According to these accounts, is the baptism in the
  Spirit a definite experience (i.e. would you know if
  you'd had it)?
- Read Acts 1:8. When the Spirit comes on
  Christians what do they receive? For what reason?

- Look up the following verses and write in your notebook what Jesus promised that the Holy Spirit would do for us.
  - John 14:26;
  - John 15:26;
  - John 16:8;
  - John 16:13;
  - John 16:14.
- Do these verses tell you that the Spirit is a 'he' or an 'it'? What difference does it make?

➔ To consider

- Read Acts 2:38–39. Was the promise of the Spirit only meant for the New Testament believers, or does it apply to you too?

The baptism of the Holy Spirit is not a reward for trying so well on our own. It is a gift to enable you to overcome right from the start!

Terry Virgo

6

How Thirsty Are You?

On the last and greatest day of the Feast, Jesus stood and said in a loud voice, 'If anyone is thirsty, let him come to me and drink. Whoever believes in me, as the Scripture has said, streams of living water will flow from within him.' By this he meant the Spirit. (John 7:37–39)

'Did you receive the Holy Spirit when you believed?' That's what Paul asked the group of Ephesians he met (Acts 19:2). Clearly he expected them to know whether they had been filled or not.

If Paul asked you the same question, how would you reply? Maybe you would say, 'Yes. God's Spirit came on me. It was great!' Or maybe you would respond, 'Well, I haven't had a definite experience, so I suppose the answer's no.'

New Christians who haven't received the baptism in the Spirit can be tempted to think, 'I'm not holy enough, special enough or clever enough, so this can't possibly be for me.' But Jesus doesn't invite only the holy, special or clever people. He invites the thirsty.

Perhaps you're thinking, 'I'm thirsty for more of God.

So how do I receive the Spirit?' Jesus tells you: 'Come to me and drink.' He doesn't say, 'Grovel before me and plead' – as if he were reluctant to part with the gift. The baptism in the Spirit is his idea. He wants you to receive it. So ask him for it and he will give it to you.

Faith plays an important part in all this. Jesus said, 'Whoever believes in me . . .' When you come to him, you must resist the temptation to be passive and just wait for something to happen. Jesus wants you to respond to him with action. How about speaking in tongues? Although you can be baptised in the Spirit and not use this gift, it is a real encouragement to you that Jesus has answered your prayer.

Many people are frightened by the idea of speaking in tongues. 'What's the point of it?' they say. 'It's a load of gibberish.' But it isn't a frightening experience. Christians who use the gift may not be able to understand what they are saying, but they know God does. By faith they believe they're expressing praises to him in a heavenly language that he loves to hear.

There is a Bible story about a widow who nearly ran out of oil. A prophet told her to pour what she had into as many jars as she could find. She probably thought, 'That's daft!' But when she began pouring, the oil flowed and filled all the containers. The miracle wasn't that the oil started, but that it kept going.

The gift of tongues isn't automatic – you have to speak the words using your own voice. At first you'll probably think, 'This is crazy. I'm making it all up.' But keep believing. You start and the oil will flow.

→ Food for thought

Jesus satisfies people who thirst for him.

- 'Come, all you who are thirsty, come to the waters; and you who have no money, come, buy and eat!' (Isaiah 55:1).
- 'Blessed are those who hunger and thirst for righteousness, for they will be filled' (Matthew 5:6).
- 'Whoever drinks the water I give him will never thirst' (John 4:14).
- 'Whoever is thirsty, let him come; and whoever wishes, let him take the free gift of the water of life' (Revelation 22:17).

→ To discover

- How did people know when Christians were filled with the Holy Spirit? Find out by looking at these verses:
  - Acts 2:1–4;
  - Acts 10:44–48;
  - Acts 19:1–7.
- From these verses, do you understand that the Spirit is released from within Christians or comes down upon them?

→ To consider

- Read Luke 11:9–13. What must you do to receive the Holy Spirit? If you'd like to receive the fullness of the Holy Spirit, reach out in faith today. You may prefer to ask another Christian to lay hands on you.

- Read 1 Corinthians 14:1,4,14. What do these verses tell you about speaking in tongues? If you've been baptised in the Spirit but haven't spoken in tongues, seek God for this gift.

[A famous tennis player] wins most of his games because he understands that the most important part of lawn tennis is the power to serve! As Christians we need to grasp that the Holy Spirit has not been given primarily to make us feel good but to equip us with power to serve.

Stephen Gaukroger

7

The Gifts of the Spirit

> Just as each of us has one body with many members, and
> these members do not all have the same function, so in
> Christ we who are many form one body, and each member
> belongs to all the others. We have different gifts, according
> to the grace given us. (Romans 12:4–6)

Just suppose that one day your right ear becomes
jealous of your mouth. 'From now on, the food's going
through me,' it informs the hands'. So all teeth are made
redundant and the tongue is on shorter hours. At dinner
time the stomach protests that nothing seems to be
appearing, limbs complain that they haven't got any
energy, and the right ear can't hear properly! There is
universal suffering when even one part fails to do what
it has been designed to do.

The Bible describes the church as the body of Christ.
The Holy Spirit gives one or more gifts to every
Christian and wants us to use them for the good of
others, so that the church will grow strong. If we opt
out, or try to take someone else's place, the whole
church will suffer.

There is at least one gift for you. You can't earn it and you don't deserve it. So you can't say, 'I've got this because I'm better than others.' In fact, the Spirit sometimes gives very prominent gifts to very weak people. That's because they depend on him rather than on their own intelligence or abilities.

When you're trying to find out what the Spirit has given you, it's good to remember that the Bible doesn't list every single gift that's available. It often focuses on general headings. Just as the word 'flower' covers hundreds of varieties, so each gift can be expressed in many different ways. Once you think you know your general area of service, you can see more clearly what God wants you to do.

How do you discover what gifts God has for you? First, ask him to show you, and then ask a Christian friend to pray with you. If you've started going to a house group, why not ask the people there to tell you what kinds of gifts they see developing in you. If the church has a 'discover your gifts' form, fill one in and pray about the result. Don't feel that you'll be using the same gifts in twenty years' time. The Spirit may have something else for you to do then.

It may not be immediately obvious what gifts God has for you, but don't just sit back and wait. Do something – however small it may seem. Offer to babysit for a single parent; visit an elderly person; invite someone round for a meal or coffee; go out with the evangelism team; pray for the sick; volunteer for things. Once you start reaching out in love to others, the areas in which God has gifted you will probably become clear.

➔ Food for thought

All Christians are part of Christ's body.

- 'The body is a unit, though it is made up of many parts; and though all its parts are many, they form one body. So it is with Christ. For we were all baptised by one Spirit into one body' (1 Corinthians 12:12–13).
- 'From [Christ] the whole body . . . grows and builds itself up in love, as each part does its work' (Ephesians 4:16).
- '[Christ] is the head of the body, the church' (Colossians 1:18).

➔ To discover

- Read 1 Corinthians 12:4–11. To find out how these nine gifts of the Spirit operate, look up the following verses:

  Gifts of revelation:
  - Matthew 22:17–22 (message of wisdom);
  - Acts 5:1–6 (message of knowledge);
  - Acts 16:16–18 (distinguishing between spirits).

  Vocal gifts:
  - Acts 11:27–28 (prophecy);
  - Acts 2:4 (tongues);
  - 1 Corinthians 14:13 (interpretation of tongues).

  Gifts of power:
  - Acts 14:8–10 (faith);
  - Acts 3:1–10 (healing);
  - Matthew 14:13–21 (miraculous powers).

⮕ To consider

- Read Romans 12:6–8 and 1 Corinthians 12:27–31. Start asking God what gifts he wants you to use.
- Pray about this with a Christian friend, and ask him/her to explain any of the gifts that you don't fully understand.
- Even if you're not a member of the church yet, you could still do something to help others in the church (e.g. serve coffee after the morning service, move chairs, do the shopping for an elderly person, etc.). Pray about this and do something.

The fruit of the Spirit was never intended to be a demonstration of our dedication and resolve. It is the evidence of our dependency on and sensitivity to the promptings of the Spirit.

Charles Stanley

8

The Fruit of the Spirit

The fruit of the Spirit is love, joy, peace, patience, kindness, goodness, faithfulness, gentleness and self-control. (Galatians 5:22–23)

We look at the future and think, 'I'd like to do this and that with my life.' Our plans are important to God – and he wants to be involved in them – but his goal for us is higher than ours. We focus mainly on what we do; he's more concerned about who we are. His greatest desire isn't to turn us into workers, but to make us like his Son.

God wants to see Christ's character in you. When you became a Christian, Jesus gave you his righteousness, but he didn't transform your character. You don't always reflect his humility or patience, kindness or compassion. You don't always say the things he'd say, or do the things he'd do. Righteousness is instant, but Christlikeness is a lifelong process.

Jesus was perfect in love, joy, peace, patience, kindness, goodness, faithfulness, gentleness and self-control. These qualities are called the 'fruit of the Spirit'. Why 'fruit' and not 'fruits'? Because they belong together – we should be cultivating them all. Why 'of the Spirit'? Because it's the Spirit who produces them. We can't manufacture an apple, a pear or a banana. We sow a seed, which grows into a tree, and in time we get the fruit. In the same way, we can't strive to get love, joy and peace, etc. We obey the Spirit, he produces the fruit in us and we become more like Christ.

So how does this work in practice? Well, let's say you are tempted to sin. 'I really want to do that,' you think, and try to justify it. The trouble is, you can hear an inner voice whispering, 'No! Don't give in to it.' That's the Spirit working on your conscience, telling you that what you want isn't right. He'll give you the power to resist the temptation, but he can't force you to obey him. You choose whether you respond to him and 'walk by the Spirit' or ignore him and 'carry out the desire of the flesh' (Galatians 5:16).

Now if you ignore the Spirit on a day-to-day basis, you won't develop his fruit. You may have the most amazing spiritual gifts, but you'll lack the character of Christ. In time, you may even find that you lose the ability to work out what's right and what's wrong because you are no longer sensitive to the Spirit.

But if you refuse to listen to your fleshly desires and always try to obey the Spirit, you'll notice that you are changing. The fruit that you didn't have will appear in your life, and you'll gradually become more like Jesus. Those God foreknew he also predestined to be conformed to the likeness of his Son, that he might be the firstborn among many brothers (Romans 8:29).

➔ Food for thought

God wants us to be fruitful.

- 'Produce fruit in keeping with repentance' (Matthew 3:8).
- 'He cuts off every branch in me that bears no fruit, while every branch that does bear fruit he prunes so that it will be even more fruitful' (John 15:2).
- 'The fruit of the light consists in all goodness, righteousness and truth' (Ephesians 5:9).
- 'Be . . . filled with the fruit of righteousness' (Philippians 1:11).

➔ To discover

- Read the following passages and write in your notebook which fruit of the Spirit you can see in operation in Jesus' life (there may be more than one fruit in each case):
  - Matthew 8:1–3;
  - Mark 10:13–16;
  - Luke 7:11–15;
  - Luke 10:21;
  - Luke 22:47–51;
  - John 14:1–3.
- Are you facing a situation in which you need the fruit of the Spirit? Which fruit in particular? How are you going to demonstrate it?

→ To consider

- Read Galatians 5:19–21. Consider these sins one by one and ask God to show you whether you're involved in any of them. If you are, confess them to God, receive his forgiveness and ask him to help you not to get involved in them again.
- Which is of greater importance to you: what you do with your life or how you can become more like Jesus?
- Do you think that if you focus on being more Christlike, God will take care of the future for you?

There is no better fuel for service that burns longer and provides more energy than love.

Donald S. Whitney

9

Follow the Way of Love

Love is patient, love is kind. It does not envy, it does not boast, it is not proud. It is not rude, it is not self-seeking, it is not easily angered, it keeps no record of wrongs. Love does not delight in evil but rejoices with the truth. It always protects, always trusts, always hopes, always perseveres. Love never fails. (1 Corinthians 13:4–8)

Follow the way of love. (1 Corinthians 14:1)

Love is the first fruit of the Spirit because it's the key to all the rest. If you are not loving, you'll never be joyful, peaceful, patient . . . . It's useless saying, 'Lord, make me a kinder person,' if you're unloving. Love others and you'll always be kind to them. Follow the way of love and the other fruit will be added too.

Paul explains the qualities of love in 1 Corinthians 13:4–8. It is patient, kind and not envious. When people treat us badly, we naturally want to lash out at them. 'I'm really hurt,' we think. 'He/she can't get away with that.' But love doesn't seek revenge and gnash its teeth enviously at the wicked. It holds back and expresses kindness, even when that kindness is undeserved.

It doesn't boast, and isn't proud, rude or self-seeking. Sometimes we may be in a senior position to others. It is tempting then to think, 'They should look up to me,' and to start ordering them around. But love doesn't act arrogantly or selfishly. It is humble and has the interests of others at heart.

It isn't easily angered and keeps no record of wrongs. On occasions someone in a senior position may be getting the credit for what we are doing. 'It's totally unfair,' we think, and feel very angry. Although love recognises injustice, it refuses to be provoked. So instead of gathering ammunition against an individual, it repeatedly overlooks personal offence.

It doesn't delight in evil, but rejoices with the truth. When we see someone doing something 'wrong' we are often quick to judge him. 'How terrible!' we think, and talk about his sin. But love doesn't condemn; it tries hard to interpret the action in a more positive way. It enjoys focusing more on good than on evil.

It always protects, trusts and hopes. We tend to judge others too quickly. Love accepts that they're not perfect and readily excuses their faults. It prays God's greatest blessing on them and treats its worst enemies as though they were its best friends.

It always perseveres and never fails. When we are in a difficult situation, we may protest and try to rebel. But love endures hardship and leaves everything in the hands of God. He isn't blind. He knows exactly what is happening and he will vindicate us in his time. Our job is not to battle for our rights, but to show love – the quality of love that only the Holy Spirit can produce in us; the love that never fails.

→ Food for thought

Love is the mark of being born again.

- 'By this all men will know that you are my disciples, if you love one another' (John 13:35).
- 'Let us love one another, for love comes from God. Everyone who loves has been born of God and knows God' (1 John 4:7).
- 'Love one another deeply from the heart. For you have been born again . . . through the living and enduring word of God' (1 Peter 1:22–23).

→ To discover

- Read Romans 5:6–8. Did Jesus wait until we were lovable before he died for us?
- Read Matthew 5:43–48. Does Jesus want us to wait for others to be lovable before we love them? Pray for someone you find it hard to love. Ask God to bless him or her.
- Read John 15:13. How do you know that Jesus loves you? If you find it hard to give and receive love, ask God to help you, and if necessary, talk this through with a Christian friend.

→ To consider

- Draw a line down a page in your notebook (it probably needs to be closer to the left-hand side than the centre). On the left of the line, write down the individual qualities of love (1 Corinthians 13:4–8) one under another, with several lines between them.

- Consider each quality in turn and ask God to show you how you could demonstrate it more.
- On the right of the line, note down what you feel he's saying to you. (*Note*: Don't strive to produce this fruit. Listen to what God says, and pray that the Spirit will produce the fruit in you naturally.)

How many times have you heard people say, 'Let's go to church'? First century believers didn't say, 'We're going to church.' They said, 'We are the church.' The church of Jesus Christ is us! Don't speak of it as a building. Jesus never did.

Charles Colson

10

I Will Build My Church

'I will build my church, and the gates of Hades will not overcome it.' (Matthew 16:18)

Mention 'church' to someone, and you're almost guaranteed to get a negative response. Church is a cold grey stone building with pews and pulpit. It is boring services and a handful of elderly people. It is jumble sales and a 'restore the steeple' fund that has been running for ages. When Jesus said, 'I will build my church,' is this what he meant?

Never! The sort of church he planned was like the one in the New Testament: not statues and steeples, but people and power. The church there is Christians loving and serving one another; praising God and praying together; prophesying and speaking in tongues; healing the sick and bringing hundreds to Christ. That's the church Jesus wants today.

You already belong to the church. When you were born again, Jesus brought you into his worldwide family. Your new brothers and sisters come from all races, tribes, languages, cultures, colours and classes.

They love Jesus and they are learning to love one another too.

You may ask, 'If I'm already in the church world-wide, why do I need to be in a local church too?' The simple answer is that you not only belong to God, you belong to others as well. If the church is a body, the different parts should be attached and working together. If the church is also a family, the members should be spending time enjoying one another's company.

God has given you a special job to do. Unless you join a local church, how will you do it? How will you use the gifts he has given you to build up other believers? And how will you cope when things get tough and you need Christians to help and encourage you? We need Jesus and each other. So it's vital for us to meet together.

When believers meet, they demonstrate to the local community what the church is really all about. Outsiders expect to see something pathetic, not something dynamic. When they walk into our meetings, we want them to think, 'Hey, this is different!' When they see our love for one another, we want them to say, 'I've never seen anything like this.' And when they hear us telling them about Jesus, we want them to ask, 'How can I know him too?'

Jesus promised, 'I will build my church' – not some trivial organisation, but a loving and powerful people. He wants you to belong to the local church and to build it with him. What do you say to that?

→ Food for thought

God's people are joined together.

- 'There is neither Jew nor Greek, slave nor free, male nor female, for you are all one in Christ Jesus' (Galatians 3:28).
- 'In [Christ] the whole building is joined together and rises to become a holy temple in the Lord. And in him you too are being built together to become a dwelling in which God lives by his Spirit' (Ephesians 2:21–22).
- 'You also, like living stones, are being built into a spiritual house' (1 Peter 2:5).

→ To discover

- Read the following:
  - Galatians 6:10;
  - Ephesians 1:5;
  - Ephesians 3:14–15;
  - Hebrews 2:11;
  - 1 John 3:1.

  These verses tell you that God has brought you into his family. In your notebook, write down why the family is such a good picture of the church, and how people in God's family should relate together.
- Read Acts 2:41 and note the order of events:
  - people became Christians;
  - they were baptised;
  - they were added to the local church.

- Read the following verses which tell you that there were local churches in several different places:
  - 1 Corinthians 1:2;
  - Galatians 1:2;
  - 1 Thessalonians 1:1.

⊡ To consider

- Read Matthew 16:13–18. Christianity is far more than just 'Jesus and me'. When Peter made his confession, Jesus didn't focus solely on him, he introduced the church. When we confess Christ, God doesn't leave us to get on with things alone – he immediately brings us into his church.

What we need to grasp clearly is a vision of the church as God has revealed it to us in the Scriptures. If we then act upon that vision, with patient and persistent prayer and with plenty of hard work, we – and others – will see the reality and glory of God once again in our midst.

David Watson

11

Which Church?

They devoted themselves to the apostles' teaching and to
the fellowship, to the breaking of bread and to prayer . . .
All the believers were together and had everything in
common. Selling their possessions and goods, they gave to
anyone as he had need. Every day they continued to meet
together in the temple courts. They broke bread in their
homes and ate together with glad and sincere hearts, praising God and enjoying the favour of all the people. (Acts
2:42–47)

Once you have decided to join a local church, which
will it be? The closest? The liveliest? The friendliest?
Does it matter? And if it does, how do you choose?

If you're looking for a perfect church, you can give up
now! Christians may have been forgiven by Jesus, but
they still make mistakes. Even the New Testament
church wasn't perfect, but it's the best model we have.
Look for a church that fits the biblical pattern most
closely. Here, and in the next study, is the pattern:

First, the Bible will be central. The early Christians
had only the Old Testament, but the apostles taught

them about Jesus and how he wanted them to live. They carefully read the letters that the apostles wrote and lived out what they were learning. Those letters are now part of our New Testament.

A good church will believe that the Bible is the word of God. When you go to a service, the preacher won't give his own ideas, he will focus on what God says. Many of the congregation will have Bibles open on their laps, and they'll take notes when he is speaking. You will get the impression that they're not just listening to the word, but that they really want to live by it.

Second, fellowship (friendship) will be important. The New Testament Christians loved each other like members of a family. They spent time together and shared meals. They even sold their possessions to meet each other's needs. Church isn't just on Sundays. The members will see each other during the week – for meals or at house-group meetings. When one person is in need, others will offer practical help.

Third, they'll take bread and wine just as Jesus commanded. The early church obeyed him and broke bread in one another's homes. In a biblical church, breaking bread isn't a formal and sombre Sunday occasion. It's a celebration of Christ's love which believers can enjoy in their homes. While they will remember Christ's sufferings, they'll also recall his resurrection and look forward to his return.

Fourth, there will be a strong emphasis on prayer. The New Testament believers prayed a lot – both alone and in groups. Why? Because God says that if we pray, he will act. You'll know if prayer is important by looking at the prayer meeting. Is there one? Is it well attended? And is it lively? You should sense that prayer is vital to the growth of the church.

➜ Food for thought

The early church was very loving.

- 'All the believers were one in heart and mind. No-one claimed that any of his possessions was his own, but they shared everything they had . . . There were no needy persons among them' (Acts 4:32,34).
- 'We loved you so much that we were delighted to share with you not only the gospel of God but our lives as well, because you had become so dear to us' (1 Thessalonians 2:8).

➜ To discover

- Read Luke 18:1–8 and answer the following questions in your notebook:
  - What is the purpose of this parable (v.1)?
  - What did the widow want (v.3)?
  - What made the judge change his mind (vv.4–5)?
  - Who do the judge and the widow represent (vv.6–7)?
  - What will we sometimes have to do (v.7)?
  - What will God eventually do for us (v.7)?
  - What does God want you to keep praying about?
- Read 1 Corinthians 11:17–34:
  - What do the bread and wine represent (vv.24–25)?

- Until when do we break bread (v.26)?
- What should we do before we break bread (v.28)?

➡ To consider

● Read Acts 2:42–47. When we follow the biblical pattern, what two reactions can we expect?

Paul tells us to 'offer your bodies as living sacrifices' (Romans 12:1). The writer of Hebrews adds, 'let us continually offer to God a sacrifice of praise' (Hebrews 13:15). In other words, worship is to permeate all we do – all the time.

Mark Altrogge

12

A Worshipping Church

'The true worshippers will worship the Father in spirit and truth, for they are the kind of worshippers the Father seeks. God is spirit, and his worshippers must worship in spirit and in truth.' (John 4:23–24)

It happens quite often. People walk into a church service expecting it to be rather traditional, but they find it lively and spontaneous. They look around in amazement. How come these Christians are so happy? They're not just singing songs, they're really worshipping God.

What is the chief mark of a biblical church? The answer is worship. Paul says that true believers worship by the Spirit, glory in Christ and put no confidence in the flesh (Philippians 3:2–3). Spirit-inspired worship is top of his list. So don't join a church just because it has a good pastor or youth group. Join it because you know that the people worship by the Spirit.

God seeks more than worship: he's really after worshippers. And he would like you to be one of them. Worshippers don't just worship on Sundays; they worship God every day. Worship characterises their lives. If you really want to be a worshipper, you'll need to know that worship involves your mind, heart, body and will.

Mind. The more you know about someone, the longer you can praise him. God wants you to know him through the Bible. The more you read it, the better you will know him, and the deeper your worship will be. When you've done something wrong, you will probably think that you can't approach God to worship him. That's not true. If you've been born again, you are righteous in Christ and have permanent access to the throne.

You need to work out what is happening in worship. If you're singing, are the words of the song directed to God, to others or to you? If you're praising God, you gaze heavenwards. If you're singing to others, you look at them.

Heart. Worship involves your heart. Maybe you find it hard to express emotion. You like the spontaneous style of worship, but struggle with the idea of shouting to God with cries of joy (Psalm 47:1). 'Isn't that embarrassing?' you think. No. It's biblical! God wants you to break through your reserve. He is worthy of lively praise.

Body. People in the Bible worshipped God by singing, clapping, shouting, dancing, kneeling and even laughing. God wants you to do these things. Praise is enjoyable. Why not enjoy it?

Will. Worship is more than just praising God; it is about yielding to him too. It's about saying, 'Lord, I'm going to do your will, regardless of the cost.' God loves to hear that. It's the best expression of worship you can ever offer him.

→ Food for thought

The best worship is in yielded lives.

● 'Job got up and tore his robe and shaved his head.
  Then he fell to the ground in worship and said . . .
  "The Lord gave and the Lord has taken away; may
  the name of the Lord be praised"' (Job 1:20–21).
● '[Jesus] fell with his face to the ground and prayed,
  "My Father, if it is possible, may this cup be taken
  from me. Yet not as I will, but as you will"' (Matthew
  26:39).

→ To discover

● Read 2 Samuel 6:13–23. In your notebook, write
  down the answers to the following questions:
  – How did Michal react to David's enthusiastic
    worship?
  – How did David respond to her?
  – What warning is there here?
  – Did David worry what people thought of him
    when he worshipped?
  – Do you worry what people think of you when
    you worship?
  – Should you?
● Look up the following verses and write down the
  ways in which people expressed their worship to
  God.
  – 2 Samuel 6:14–15;
  – Psalm 63:4;
  – Psalm 95:2,6;
  – Psalm 126:2.

⊡ To consider

- Pray that God will give you sensitivity to the Spirit in the worship meetings.
- When you're worshipping, use your mind. Think about what you're singing. Try to discern if the Spirit is highlighting a theme (e.g. God's faithfulness, his love, his power, his goodness, etc.).
- Begin to worship God in new ways. You might prefer to start in private and then become more public.

There are three kinds of giving: grudge giving, duty giving and thanks giving. Grudge giving says, 'I hate to'; duty giving says, 'I ought to'; thanks giving says, 'I want to'.

Robert Rodenmayer

13
Give, and It Will Be Given

'The ground of a certain rich man produced a good crop
. . . he said, ". . . I will tear down my barns and build bigger
ones, and there I will store all my grain and my goods. And
I'll say to myself, 'You have plenty of good things laid up
for many years. Take life easy; eat, drink and be merry.'"'
(Luke 12:16,18–19)

Many rich people threw in large amounts. But a poor
widow came and put in two very small copper coins, worth
only a fraction of a penny . . . Jesus said, '. . . They all gave
out of their wealth; but she, out of her poverty, put in everything – all she had to live on.' (Mark 12:41–42,44)

Many of us struggle with the idea of giving. Why?
Because we have been conditioned to hold back. 'If I
give, I won't have enough for my own needs,' we think.
So we cling to our money and possessions. The more
wealth we have, the more secure we feel, and the more
materialistic we become.

It's quite a shock, then, when we read what Jesus says
about riches, because he turns everything we've
believed on its head. Look at the story of the rich man

who built bigger barns for his crops. The world would honour someone like that. He was planning for a cosy future, but God called him a fool! His problems were independence and pride. He lived for now and forgot that one day he would die. That's why he was a fool.

Then there is the example of the poor widow. She put everything she had into the temple treasury. What would people say about that? 'What a fool!' But Jesus praised her devotion. She wasn't amassing wealth in this life. She was storing up treasure in heaven.

Jesus said: 'Give, and it will be given to you' (Luke 6:38). Our immediate reaction is, 'That's crazy! It can't possibly work.' But it does. Many Christians have proved it. Some of them don't have much to start with, but they give what they can to God's work, and he rewards them. Their motivation isn't reward, nor do they think, 'The church leaders expect me to give, so I'd better obey.' They simply recall how much Jesus gave for them and want to give all they can to him.

So how much do we give? In the Old Testament, God's people gave a tithe (a tenth). Tithing your income is a good starting point, and your local church is the best place to give your money, because then you can see where it's going and can feel personally involved. Don't let your tithing become mechanical. God wants you to be motivated by love – and that may mean that sometimes you'll tithe, and then feel so moved by someone's need or a Christian project that you'll give again.

Do you admire the rich fool or the poor widow? Which are you imitating? If you decide to follow the widow's example, people will call you a fool. But they're living for now, and one day all their wealth will be destroyed. Surely it's not foolish to pour your life into something that is going to last for ever.

➔ Food for thought

God blesses givers.

- 'Give, and it will be given to you. A good measure, pressed down, shaken together and running over, will be poured into your lap. For with the measure you use, it will be measured to you' (Luke 6:38).
- 'Sell your possessions and give to the poor. Provide purses for yourselves that will not wear out, a treasure in heaven that will not be exhausted' (Luke 12:33).

➔ To discover

- Read 2 Corinthians 9:6–15. In your notebook write down:
  - the meaning of verse 6;
  - how we should give (v.7);
  - how we should not give (v.7);
  - what God promises to do for givers (vv.8–11);
  - how people will react to your generosity (vv.12–14);
  - who God's 'indescribable gift' is (v.15).

➔ To consider

- Read Matthew 6:24. Pray that God will help you to put your security in him rather than in money and possessions.

- Read Malachi 3:8–10. God promises that if we give to him, he will give to us. He even tells us to test him in this. If you are struggling financially, talk to one of your church leaders. But don't excuse yourself from giving.

The Holy Scriptures tell us what we could never learn any other way: They tell us what we are, who we are, how we got here, why we are here, and what we are required to do while we remain here.

A. W. Tozer

14

The Word of God

For the word of God is living and active. Sharper than any double-edged sword, it penetrates even to dividing soul and spirit, joints and marrow; it judges the thoughts and attitudes of the heart. (Hebrews 4:12)

Before we became Christians, many of us saw the Bible as a boring history book. 'It contains plenty of interesting moral teaching,' we thought, 'but you can't believe it all. It's full of contradictions and impossible miracles, and it's irrelevant to people today.'

Then we were born again, and we soon realised that people were actually taking the Bible seriously. They weren't only reading it, but trying to live by it. And we somehow felt that we should be doing the same.

So why do Christians read the Bible? Is it because Bible reading is a good thing to do? No. It's because the Bible is the word of God. In that sense, it is 'living and active'. We read and the living God speaks to us. He tells us about himself and shows us how to live. If it's that important, how can we get the most out of it?

Well, for a start, how about making a few enquiries

and buying or borrowing some books that will explain
about Bible stud   Why not get a study guide and work
through one of the books in the Bible? Don't start with
a difficult book like Leviticus or Revelation. Try Luke,
Acts or Psalms. And don't read the Scriptures casually
as you might a novel. Be humble. Before you start, ask
the Holy Spirit to help you to understand, and expect
God to speak to you.

Start at chapter 1. Read a sec on and think about it
for a while. What does it mean? What is God saying to
you? Does he want you to do something? Write down
what he says to you. Don't worry if you don't understand everything. You can find out about the difficult
things later. Read the passage again – God may show
you something you've missed.

At the end of your study, meditate on (think about) the
verse that is saying the most to you. Then apply it to the
tasks or pressures that lie ahead, and talk to God about
them. You might even write down the verse and try to
learn it during the day. Work through the entire book
and then begin on another.

Bible study is satisfying only when you allow God to
speak to you personally through the word. The overall
goal is not to be able to say, 'I've read the whole Bible
in a year,' but, 'I know God better and he's changing
me.'

He wants us to have an intimate personal relationship
with him, but he won't respond to casual enquirers. He
will reveal himself to those who are seeking him with
all their heart.

→ Food for thought

We must do what God says.

- 'Everyone who hears these words of mine and puts them into practice is like a wise man' (Matthew 7:24).
- 'Do not merely listen to the word, and so deceive yourselves. Do what it says' (James 1:22).
- 'The man who says, "I know him," but does not do what he commands is a liar . . . But if anyone obeys his word, God's love is truly made complete in him' (1 John 2:4–5).

→ To discover

- Read Joshua 1:8. How do we become successful?
- Read Psalm 119:1–16 and write down in your notebook what the psalmist says about God's word (law, statutes, etc.).
- Read 2 Timothy 3:15–17.
  - What can Bible reading do (v.15)?
  - All Scripture is what (v.16)?
  - What is the Bible useful for (v.16)?
  - What is the goal (v.17)?

→ To consider

- Are you reading this book in a disciplined way, or is it rather haphazard? Choose a good time and a quiet place to meet with God and don't let interruptions cut across that time.

- Decide which book of the Bible you want to study when you've finished this book.
- Decide how long you want to study for each day (you'll probably need about half an hour).

Prayer, like air, water and food, is necessary for our survival and growth . . . Prayer doesn't have to be a duty; it can be a delight.

Larry Lea

15

Lord, Teach Us to Pray

Very early in the morning, while it was still dark, Jesus got up, left the house and went off to a solitary place, where he prayed. (Mark 1:35)

One day Jesus was praying in a certain place. When he finished, one of his disciples said to him, 'Lord, teach us to pray, just as John taught his disciples.' (Luke 11:1)

Mark's Gospel outlines a day in the life of Jesus. First we see him preaching in the synagogue and casting out an evil spirit. Then he goes to Simon's house and releases his mother-in-law from a fever. And in the evening the whole town gathers at the door to receive his teaching, healing or deliverance (Mark 1:21–34). The next morning we would expect Jesus to have a lie in and recover quietly. Instead, he goes off to pray (Mark 1:35).

Even though Jesus was God's Son, he still set aside time to pray. We read, 'Crowds of people came . . . But Jesus often withdrew to lonely places and prayed' (Luke 5:15–16). The disciples watched him. They heard his powerful teaching and saw his miracles. And they soon recognised that there was a link between his power and his prayer. And they realised that if they were going to be effective, they would have to learn how to pray.

Many Christians have made this connection too. They want God to use them powerfully and they know that they need to have a personal prayer life. But they are unsure about how to pray. Some of them develop their own formula, but although their prayers do work, there's a far better way.

The disciples instinctively knew that they needed to be shown how to pray. So they didn't try to work out their own prayer plan. They went to the expert: Jesus himself. There was no one better to ask, and there was no better answer than the one he gave. 'Pray like this . . .' he said, and gave them a prayer framework which we now know as the 'Lord's Prayer'.

Many of us learned the Lord's Prayer as children, or heard it recited in church services. People always raced through it and we became convinced that Jesus actually expected us to reel it off like parrots. But that was never his intention. His plan was to provide us with a structure which would help us to concentrate better when we prayed. The phrases weren't meant to be repeated mindlessly, but treated as headings which we could expand ourselves.

Jesus wants you to have the same sort of impact that he had when he was on earth. So he invites you to pray in the way he directed his disciples. Over the next few studies we will be looking at the Lord's Prayer and learning how to pray it. We'll also be focusing on the subjects that are mentioned in the Lord's Prayer and applying them to our lives.

⮕ Food for thought

God listens when we pray.

- 'He hears my voice' (Psalm 55:17).
- 'The eyes of the Lord are on the righteous and his ears are attentive to their cry' (Psalm 34:15).
- 'He fulfils the desires of those who fear him; he hears their cry and saves them' (Psalm 145:19).
- 'This is the confidence we have in approaching God: that if we ask anything according to his will, he hears us' (1 John 5:14).

⮕ To discover

- Read Matthew 6:5–13 and write down in your notebook the answers to the following questions:
  - How do hypocrites pray (v. 5)?
  - What 'reward' do you think they receive?
  - How should we pray (v. 6)?
  - What will God do for those who pray like this (v. 6)?
  - What must we avoid (v. 7)?
- Read Philippians 4:6–7. Consider the thing that gives you most anxiety. Do exactly what verse 6 tells you to do. Then receive the promise of verse 7. See if you can memorise these verses over the next few days.

⮕ To consider

- You may be wondering whether there is a 'right

posture' for prayer. The answer is 'no'. You can kneel, sit, stand, walk round the room, or lie prostrate on the floor. The important thing is that you're communicating with God.

- Remember that prayer is a two-way process, so try to hear what God is saying too. Don't worry if it's all strange to start with. You'll get used to it.

Abba and imma – daddy and mummy – are the first words Jewish children learn to speak. And abba is so personal, so familiar a term that no one ever dared to use it in address to the great God of the universe – no one until Jesus.

Richard Foster

16

Our Father in Heaven

'Our Father in heaven.' (Matthew 6:9)

To all who received him, to those who believed in his name, he gave the right to become children of God. (John 1:12)

Many people find it hard to relate to God as their Father. 'My earthly father treated me badly,' they think. 'I don't want to see God in the same role.' To protect themselves they 'play safe'. They accept with their minds that God loves them, but they refuse to let him get any closer. That would be too risky.

Jesus' earthly relationship with his Father was good because it was based on love. From the start, Jesus knew that God loved and totally accepted him. His ministry flowed from this knowledge.

You are now a child of God, and he wants you to understand from the beginning of your Christian life that he loves and totally accepts you. Once you realise this, you'll relax in his love and allow him to use you. You'll also trust him whatever happens. But if you don't believe that God loves you, you'll be suspicious of him. Then you'll become fearful and anxious and will act independently of him.

There are two ways in which you can do this. First, you can think that the world offers you much more excitement than God. 'I'm missing out,' you conclude. 'My unbelieving friends are having far more fun than I am!' So after a while you turn your back on God and begin to seek satisfaction in other things.

Second, you can decide to continue with God, but fall into the trap of serving him in a dutiful way. 'I must keep up the good works,' you think. 'I'm expected to plod on with my Bible study, prayer and helping others.' So you do these things, even though at times they almost bore you to death!

Maybe your earthly father neglected you, held things back from you, or loved you only if you performed well. God isn't like that. He promises never to leave you (Hebrews 13:5). He gives you good gifts (Matthew 7:11). And he loves you unconditionally. His love doesn't depend on whether you have prayed or done something kind for someone else. You can't make him love you any more or less than he does now. He loves you as much as he loves Jesus.

Jesus didn't teach us to pray, 'Our Master in heaven.' That's because God doesn't want us to relate to him as slaves. He isn't looking for dutiful obedience to a set of rules. He is looking for a loving relationship with his children. It will involve discipline, but that discipline will be motivated by the Spirit and spurred on by love.

➔ Food for thought

Christians are children or sons of God.

- 'You are no longer a slave, but a son' (Galatians 4:7).
- 'You did not receive a spirit that makes you a slave again to fear, but you received the Spirit of sonship. And by him we cry, "Abba, Father." The Spirit himself testifies with our spirit that we are God's children' (Romans 8:15).
- 'In love [God] predestined us to be adopted as his sons through Jesus Christ' (Ephesians 1:4–5).

➔ To discover

- Consider your relationship with your own father and see if this is affecting your relationship with God.
- During the next week or so, pray (with someone else maybe) that God will release you from any negative attitudes towards fatherhood.
- Pray too that God will help you to relate to him as your Father.

➔ To consider

- Focus on God as your Father. Consider how much he loves you by recalling Jesus' sacrifice for you. Remember that he accepts you in his Son and sees you as righteous.
- Talk to God freely and naturally about things he has done for you recently. Thank him for them.

'Great is the Lord and greatly to be praised' – not because we happen to feel great, but because he is eternally great, and therefore eternally to be praised. Moreover, whenever we honour God by giving him a sacrifice of praise, always he honours us.

David Watson

17

Hallowed Be Your Name

'Hallowed be your name . . .' (Matthew 6:9)

Great is the Lord in Zion; he is exalted over all the nations.
Let them praise your great and awesome name – he is holy.
(Psalm 99:2–3)

On one occasion Jesus prayed, 'Holy Father' (John 17:11). In doing this he brought together beautifully the awesomeness and intimacy of God. Although we begin our prayers with 'Our Father', we must understand that he isn't just Father. He is also Majestic Lord. If we over-emphasise his Fatherhood, we'll tend to drag him down to our level; but if we over-emphasise his holiness, we won't be able to lift ourselves up to his. The secret lies in balancing them so that neither outweighs the other. So what does it mean to 'hallow' God's name?

'Hallow' means 'to reverence, sanctify or keep holy'. We hallow God by praising him. Once we've drawn near to God as Father, he wants us to worship him. That can be hard – especially if we're facing real problems. It is natural then to plunge into asking him for things.

But if we do this, we'll become self-centred. Prayer isn't about presenting God with a list of personal needs, but about glorifying him. He'll honour us if we put him first.

Singing glorifies God. Sometimes we'll sing with enthusiasm, but on other occasions singing will be about the last thing we want to do. God understands our feelings and we need to remember that he knows what's happening to us and is in control of everything. And, in spite of what's going on, he is still worthy of our praise. We demonstrate our faith in him by singing worship songs or hymns which glorify him – regardless of how we are feeling.

We hallow God's name. People in the Bible were given names which said something about their characters. God's name is 'I am who I am' (Exodus 3:14). His character is rather like a diamond. It has many facets and each one says something different about him. For example, God calls himself our righteousness, our peace, our provider, our healer and our shepherd. We hallow his name by meditating on one or more of his names and turning our thoughts into declarations of faith and praise.

So one day we may decide to consider the name 'Righteousness'. 'Father,' we say, 'you are my righteousness. I praise you because Jesus died for me and has made me righteous for ever. I want to continue to hallow your name by living righteously.' The next day maybe we'll take the name 'Shepherd'. Then we'll glorify God for leading and caring for us, and say that we want to hallow his name by staying close to him.

⇥ Food for thought

We're exhorted to praise God's name.

- 'Ascribe to the Lord the glory due to his name' (Psalm 29:2).
- 'Sing the glory of his name; make his praise glorious!' (Psalm 66:2).
- 'Sing to God, sing praise to his name, extol him' (Psalm 68:4).
- 'Give thanks to him and praise his name' (Psalm 100:4).
- 'Glory in his holy name; let the hearts of those who seek the Lord rejoice' (Psalm 105:3).

⇥ To discover

- Look up the following verses and write down in your notebook the different names of God (there may be more than one name in each verse):
  - Genesis 22:14;
  - Exodus 15:2, 26;
  - Exodus 17:15;
  - Deuteronomy 33:29;
  - Judges 6:24;
  - 2 Samuel 22:2–3;
  - Psalm 23:1;
  - Isaiah 63:16;
  - Jeremiah 33:16;
  - Ezekiel 48:35;
  - John 15:5.

You can now refer back to this list when you want
to pray for God's name to be hallowed.

● Read Psalm 34:1–2.
  – When did David praise God (v.1)?
  – Should you rejoice only when you're happy?
  – When should you also rejoice (v.2)?

● Read Habakkuk 3:17–18 and note how deter-
  mined Habakkuk was to rejoice in God, no matter
  what happened to him.

➔ To consider

● Choose one of God's names and spend a short time
  thinking about it.

● Pray that God will help you to hallow his name in
  your life.

● Sing to God one or two worship songs or hymns.
  (*Note*: Some songs and hymns focus on glorifying
  God. Others refer more to the Christian life. Try to
  sing the ones that glorify God.) Alternatively, listen
  to a couple of tracks on a worship tape; dance to
  them, sing a psalm, sing in tongues, etc.

Jesus put on flesh and came to this world to free mankind from the rule of Satan. He came into this world where Satan was reigning so that He might build – accomplish and enlarge – His kingdom.

Paul Y. Cho

18

Your Kingdom Come

'Your kingdom come.' (Matthew 6:10)

Selfishness, hatred, violence, sickness, oppression and despair – that's what you see when you look around you. These are the marks of a kingdom ruled by the devil (Satan). He controls the world we live in.

Jesus came to earth to recapture a rebel planet. His mission wasn't just to bring us salvation, but to 'destroy the devil's work'. He was a 'warrior King' who would free the world from Satan's grasp by bringing a new government to earth (Isaiah 9:6) – the kingdom of God.

When we repented and believed the gospel, we entered the kingdom and began to enjoy the power of the Spirit (Hebrews 6:5). Now when we see God healing and delivering people, we know that he is destroying Satan's kingdom and establishing his own (Luke 11:20).

God has promised to give the nations to his Son (Psalm 2:6–8). That is the great purpose of history: one day Jesus will reign supreme over everything. Jesus told his disciples about this, then he said that he wanted them to rule with him (Luke 22:29). He didn't just mean 'in heaven', but 'now' (Luke 12:32).

When the seventy-two disciples went out on their preaching and healing tour, they were proclaiming the kingdom of God (Luke 10:1–20). And after the Spirit came at Pentecost, the church preached the same message and saw the same sort of miracles (Acts 8:12–13). Clearly the early believers didn't view church as a cosy club. They knew that the world was a battleground and that they were in a war.

The mission of the church hasn't changed. Jesus now wants us to establish his kingdom on earth (Matthew 10:7–8). When we pray, 'Your kingdom come,' we're asking God to fulfil his promise that Jesus will reign on earth. We are asking him to destroy the devil's work by healing people and delivering them from demons, and by drawing them to receive him as their King.

You can pray, 'Your kingdom come,' into the situations where you want to see Christ reign. Maybe there is someone in your family who isn't a Christian, or there is a disagreement at work. Maybe you want to see God move powerfully at a church youth weekend, or in a famine-torn country. Sometimes God may ask you to be involved in answering your prayer (e.g. in praying for someone who is sick). It's great when you're the one he uses to break the devil's hold.

➔ Food for thought

Christians are in a battle.

- 'I saw Satan fall like lightning from heaven. I have

given you authority to trample on snakes and scorpions and to overcome all the power of the enemy' (Luke 10:18–19).

- 'Our struggle is not against flesh and blood, but against the rulers, against the authorities, against the powers of this dark world and against the spiritual forces of evil in the heavenly realms' (Ephesians 6:12).

➔ To discover

- Pray through the earlier part of the Lord's Prayer and add 'Thy kingdom come'.
- Read Isaiah 61:1–3 and Luke 4:18–19. What are the characteristics of the kingdom?

➔ To consider

- In your notebook, write down how you want Jesus to reign in:
  - your family or friends;
  - your church;
  - your school, college, workplace, club, neighbourhood, etc;
  - the nation;
  - the wider world.
- Pray for at least one person or situation in each category. Then you won't become preoccupied with your own little world.

If we are living in disobedience and therefore out of touch with God we cannot expect to receive God's guidance, even though we may pray earnestly for it . . . We must be in right relationship with the Guide.

Arthur Wallis

19

Your Will Be Done

'Your will be done on earth as it is in heaven.' (Matthew 6:10)

Some people think God's will is something heavy. They assume he wants them to do all the things they hate; that God's will has to be endured, not enjoyed, and they've just got to get on with it.

But God doesn't want to make Christians do things they don't want to do. He has no desire to see us gritting our teeth and ploughing wearily on towards heaven where we collapse in an exhausted heap! What advertisement is this for the joyful gospel of God?

Jesus didn't see God's will as something he had to tolerate. On the contrary, it was his greatest delight. He called it his 'food' – it really satisfied him, and gave him a feeling of contentment when he'd accomplished it.

God has plans for your life. He has worked out what sort of 'food' you need, and exactly how much you can manage. He wants you to discover what his will for you is, and to enjoy doing it as much as his Son did.

So how did Jesus find out what God's will was? He

prayed. Before he chose his disciples he prayed all night (Luke 6:12–13). And in spite of his busy schedule, he 'often withdrew to lonely places and prayed' (Luke 5:16).

Many Christians have busy schedules too. But they don't stop and ask God whether what they're doing fits into his plan for them. They race around thinking they can't afford to stop, when really they can't afford to be in a hurry. God would reveal his will to them if they paused and asked him to.

Jesus knew that God's will for him was best – whether he was healing people and setting them free from demons, or facing criticism, betrayal, torture and death. No matter what the situation, he faced it with great calmness. His absolute faith in God's will for his life gave him a deep sense of peace.

God wants you to know that his will for you is 'good, pleasing and perfect' (Romans 12:2), and he invites you to do it. He'll help you by gently bringing your will into line with his (Philippians 2:13). As you respond to him, you'll find yourself wanting to do his will rather than your own.

Doing God's will involves absolute surrender. It means telling God that he knows what's best for you and releasing yourself totally into his hands. It means praying daily, 'Your will be done in my life.' And it brings the peace that Jesus enjoyed when he was on earth.

⊡ Food for thought

God wants us to know and do his will.

- 'Do not be foolish, but understand what the Lord's will is' (Ephesians 5:17).
- 'We have not stopped praying for you and asking God to fill you with the knowledge of his will' (Colossians 1:9).
- 'Epaphras . . . is always wrestling in prayer for you, that you may stand firm in all the will of God' (Colossians 4:12).
- 'May . . . God . . . equip you with everything good for doing his will' (Hebrews 13:21).

→ To discover

- Read John 4:34 and John 17:4.
- Jesus accomplished everything that God gave him to do. Pray that you too will finish the work God gives you to do.
- Pray through the earlier part of the Lord's Prayer and add, 'Your will be done on earth as it is in heaven.'

→ To consider

- Reflect on and pray about the overall direction of your life.
- Pray about specific issues where you want God's will to be done.
- Ask God to reveal to you any areas in your life where you are resisting his will. Respond to what he says.

The God who saved you and poured out the Holy Spirit for you also wants to give you daily bread . . . Seek first His kingdom and righteousness. Pray for your daily bread in the name of Jesus. Then God will supply your needs . . . He will. You don't need to worry.

Paul Y. Cho

20

Give Us Today . . .

'Give us today our daily bread.' (Matthew 6:11)

'If you, then, though you are evil, know how to give good gifts to your children, how much more will your Father in heaven give good gifts to those who ask him!' (Matthew 7:11)

God doesn't care only about your spiritual life. He wants you to know that he cares about you as a person. He made you, and like any good earthly father, he wants to look after you.

The disciples thought that Jesus was interested only in people's spiritual lives. One day he was teaching a vast crowd on a hillside. Since it was getting late, the disciples asked him to send the people away to buy food. But Jesus fed them (Matthew 14:13–21). On another occasion, Jesus cooked breakfast for his disciples (John 21:10–12). He knew that they were hungry, thirsty and tired. And he wants to meet all your needs, just as he did theirs.

God isn't a mean master. His character is described

as 'love' (1 John 4:8), and love can't hold back or remain neutral. It has to give. We might expect God to give to those who deserve to receive, but he's 'kind to the ungrateful and wicked' (Luke 6:35). And he saves people without waiting for them to improve.

We sometimes give dutifully and grudgingly, but God always gives joyfully and generously. When the prodigal son returned home, his father didn't say, 'Before I hug you, go and wash off the smell of pig. Then find some old clothes in the barn and I'll make you a toasted sandwich.' He lavished gifts on his son and prepared a banquet for him (Luke 15:22–25). That's God's attitude to giving! He loves it!

God's greatest gift is his Son, and his most basic gift is our daily bread. Surely, if God is willing to give us both the most precious and the most common things, he'll supply us with everything in between.

In the Old Testament, God wanted his people to trust him to provide for them on a daily basis, so he told them to collect enough food for one day at a time (Exodus 16:11–18). Jesus took up this theme when he taught us to pray, 'Give us today our daily bread.' He didn't mean, 'Don't save up for anything.' He meant, 'Don't hoard, because when you get comfortable, you'll be tempted not to depend on me.'

Every day Jesus wants us to pray for what we need. 'Bread' includes physical, emotional and spiritual needs. At the beginning of the day, we can look ahead and tell God how we'd like him to help us. At the end of the day, we can look back and thank him for the way he's answered our prayer.

➔ Food for thought

God loves giving to us.

- 'No good thing does he withhold from those whose walk is blameless' (Psalm 84:11).
- 'I have come that they may have life, and have it to the full' (John 10:10).
- '[God] is able to do immeasurably more than all we ask or imagine' (Ephesians 3:20).
- 'God . . . richly provides us with everything for our enjoyment' (1 Timothy 6:17).

➔ To discover

- Read Matthew 6:25–34.
  - What doesn't God want you to do (v.31)?
  - What does he want you to do (v.33)?
  - What will the result be (v.33)?
- Read Philippians 4:19 and correct the following statement: And my God might meet some of your needs according to the way he feels.

➔ To consider

- Pray through the earlier part of the Lord's Prayer and add, 'Give us this day our daily bread.'
- Look at the day that lies ahead and consider how you would like God to provide for your:
  - physical needs (e.g. food, health, strength, finance);

- emotional needs (e.g. security in God's love; peace in a difficult situation; joy when things aren't working out);
- spiritual needs (e.g. greater sensitivity to the Holy Spirit, help when you're telling a friend about Jesus).

You cannot deal with sin until you look it in the eye. Undress it. Strip off the jacket of excuses you made to cover its ugliness. Tear away shirt, pants, everything that hides its nakedness, then say, 'This is my child. I, and I alone, am responsible for it.'

John White

21

Forgive Us Our Debts

'Forgive us our debts.' (Matthew 6:12)

No-one who is born of God will continue to sin. (1 John 3:9)

Jesus resisted sin. If you're 'in him', you have the power to resist sin too. The trouble is, you won't always use it. Then you'll need to confess your sin and receive God's forgiveness.

That isn't always easy. Admitting we're wrong can be painful. It's much easier to make excuses like, 'It's my little weakness,' or, 'I'm not the type to keep to the speed limit.' When we do that, we start living by our own standards of right and wrong, then we rely on the positive things we do to see us through.

But hiding sin is actually more painful than confessing it. That is because God disciplines us if we have sin in our lives. When he sees something he wants to deal with, he tugs at it gently. If we confess it, he'll forgive us and give us his peace. But if we cling to it, we'll feel guilty until we let it go. God's discipline is 'for our good'

(Hebrews 12:10). He loves us too much to let us suffer because of unconfessed sin.

Some Christians seem to live under a cloud of condemnation. They often feel guilty, but can't explain why. They know they are very weak and they think they are always failing God. And they're often tempted to give up on themselves because they'll never be good enough.

These people haven't realised that there is a difference between the devil's condemnation and the Father's conviction. The devil loads us down with a general 'burden' of sin which has no apparent root. We feel condemned and assume that we have committed a sin. But because we can't be specific about it, we don't know what to confess.

We must reject this cloud of condemnation. We'll know if we have sinned, because God's conviction will slice into our conscience like a 'sharp double edged sword' (Hebrews 4:12). He will make sure we know if we've offended him!

God doesn't want us to be preoccupied with sin, but he does want us to be sensitive to it. We must learn to examine our lives by asking questions like, 'Am I living by the Bible?' 'Am I acting lovingly towards others?' 'Am I sinning by not doing something that God wants me to do?'

Sin isn't worth holding on to. It makes us feel guilty, then it slowly leads us into indifference or bitterness. Jesus gives us the opportunity to search our hearts and ask God to reveal what we might be doing wrong. When we confess, he will forgive. And that forgiveness will often be accompanied by a great freedom and joy.

➔ Food for thought

Sin need have no power over us.

- 'Count yourselves dead to sin but alive to God in Christ Jesus . . . You have been set free from sin and have become slaves to righteousness' (Romans 6:11,18).
- 'If Christ is in you, your body is dead because of sin, yet your spirit is alive because of righteousness' (Romans 8:10).
- 'He himself bore our sins in his body on the tree, so that we might die to sins and live for righteousness' (1 Peter 2:24).

➔ To discover

- Read 1 Samuel 16:7. What does man look at? What concerns God more?
- Read Psalm 32:3–5. Note that when David held on to his sin he felt physically, emotionally and spiritually drained.
- Now read verse 11 and note how someone feels when he knows that he's not concealing any sin.

➔ To consider

- Pray through the earlier part of the Lord's Prayer and add, 'Forgive us our debts.'
- Spend a few moments asking the Holy Spirit to reveal to you anything about you which may have offended God (e.g. have you lied, gossiped, broken

a promise, watched an unhelpful film on TV, sworn at someone, drunk too much alcohol at a party, become lazy, etc?).

● Ask God to forgive you and receive that forgiveness.

If we nurture feelings of bitterness we are little better than inmates of an internal concentration camp. We lock ourselves in a lonely isolation chamber, walled in by our own refusal to forgive.

Charles R. Swindoll

22

. . . As We Have Forgiven

'Forgive us our debts, as we also have forgiven our debtors.'
(Matthew 6:12)

As far as the east is from the west, so far has he removed
our transgressions from us. (Psalm 103:12)

'And you expect me to let him off after all he's done to
me? Why should I? He should pay for the suffering he's
caused. There's no way I can forgive him.'

That is the natural reaction to someone who's hurt
you. He (or she) should suffer as much as you have. He
doesn't deserve forgiveness, and you're justified in
being angry and resentful. As far as you're concerned,
that's the end of the matter. Jesus doesn't agree.

He taught us to pray, 'Forgive us . . . as we also
forgive.' When we pray this, we're saying, 'Lord, I
expect you to deal with me as I deal with others. Give
me the same amount of forgiveness that I give to them.'
If we want to know the freedom and joy of forgiveness,
we must forgive.

Jesus gave us a parable about forgiveness. There was

a man who owed his master millions of pounds – a sum he could never repay. He fell down before his master and begged for time to pay back the money, but the master took pity on him and released him from the debt.

You could never repay the debt of sin. You cried out to God for mercy and he forgave you. He didn't think, 'Right, you've been particularly wicked, so I'm going to delay my forgiveness. I want you to know how much you've hurt and angered me, so you can just suffer for a while and then maybe I'll think about forgiving you.' No. Immediately he heard your cry, he forgave you – completely.

The servant in the parable was forgiven, but not forgiving. He found a fellow-servant who owed him a few pounds and demanded that he pay it back. When this man pleaded for mercy, the first servant threw him into prison. Hearing this news, the master said to the first servant, 'Shouldn't you have had mercy on your fellow-servant just as I had on you?' In other words, 'Why don't you forgive as you've been forgiven?'

The master put his servant in jail for his unforgiveness. Here God warns us that if we refuse to forgive someone, our unforgiveness will actually imprison us. We may feel justified in holding on to a grudge, but it will bind us and ruin our relationship with God.

When we pray this part of the Lord's Prayer, we're accepting its terms. We're telling God that we're happy to work to the standard he's set – that in the same measure as we offer forgiveness to others, he will return forgiveness to us. Do you agree to that?

➔ Food for thought

God wants us to forgive others.

- 'When you stand praying, if you hold anything against anyone, forgive him, so that your Father in heaven may forgive you your sins' (Mark 11:25).
- 'Be kind and compassionate to one another, forgiving each other, just as in Christ God forgave you' (Ephesians 4:32).
- 'Bear with each other and forgive whatever grievances you may have against one another. Forgive as the Lord forgave you' (Colossians 3:13).

➔ To discover

- Read Luke 23:34. Write down what Jesus had to suffer from people (e.g. hatred, betrayal, desertion).
- Write down anything that you've had to suffer from people that Jesus hasn't already suffered. Forgive as he did.
- Read the parable about the master and his servants. You'll find it in Matthew 18:21–35.
- Read Matthew 6:14–15. Try to memorise these two verses over the next few days.

➔ To consider

- Pray through the earlier part of the Lord's Prayer and add, '. . . as we have forgiven our debtors.'

- Remind yourself of how much God has forgiven you.
- Ask the Holy Spirit to reveal to you if you're holding anything against anyone else.
- Forgive anyone who comes to mind.

There are situations which will be dangerous to you; watch and pray, always be on guard lest you fall into temptation.

D. Martyn Lloyd-Jones

23

Lead Us Not into Temptation

'And lead us not into temptation.' (Matthew 6:13)

God cannot be tempted by evil, nor does he tempt anyone;
but each one is tempted when, by his own evil desire, he
is dragged away and enticed. (James 1:13–14)

Every Christian will face temptation – just as Jesus did.
Temptation itself isn't sin. It's only if we give in to it that
we sin. Then, we can't blame anyone else, or even the
devil, because we are responsible for what we've done.

When Jesus teaches us to pray, 'Lead us not into
temptation,' he isn't saying, 'Pray that God won't allow
you to be tempted.' Rather, he's encouraging us, 'Be
ready! Even before you're tempted, ask God to give you
the strength to overcome.' So how do we recognise
temptation? The Bible tells us that it comes from three
main sources: the world, the flesh and the devil. We'll
look at the first two of these in this study, and at the third
in the next.

The devil has corrupted the world, and Christians are
often pressurised to conform to the standards around

them. The world says, 'To get anywhere in life you've got to be intelligent, educated, rich, married and well known.' But Jesus' assessment of success is different. 'Blessed are the poor in spirit,' he says (Matthew 5:3) and then goes on to describe people whom the world would not consider blessed at all.

We're different from unbelievers. We once belonged to the world and thought as the world does; now we belong to God and must learn to think as he does. That's why the Bible tells us, 'Do not conform to the pattern of the world, but be transformed by the renewing of your mind' (Romans 12:2). We must never allow the world's standards to invade our lifestyle.

We must master our flesh too. Although God wants us to enjoy things (1 Timothy 6:17), he doesn't want us to over-indulge in them. We're called to 'seek first his kingdom' (Matthew 6:33) – which involves an act of will. If we seek other things first, we'll eventually find ourselves being ruled by our feelings and desires.

The way to discover whether we're being controlled by our flesh is to examine how we live. For example, are we spending too much time in front of the TV, or are we going out too much? If we are, we need to confess it to God and change our priorities. God knows exactly how he wants each of us to use our time for his glory. We must fit in with his plans.

God promises that he will never let you face any temptation that is too hard for you. He will always give you grace to escape. The world and the flesh will tempt you. Pray for God's help to recognise the temptations, and to resist them.

→ Food for thought

God will help us when we're tempted.

- 'No temptation has seen you except what is common to man. And God is faithful; he will not let you be tempted beyond what you can bear. But when you are tempted, he will also provide a way out so that you can stand up under it' (1 Corinthians 10:13).
- 'Because [Jesus] suffered when he was tempted, he is able to help those who are being tempted' (Hebrews 2:18).

→ To discover

- Read Matthew 5:1–12 and write down the people Jesus says are blessed (e.g. poor in spirit, mourners).
- Pray through the earlier part of the Lord's Prayer and add, 'And lead us not into temptation.'
- Pray that today God will help you to resist the temptation:
  - to conform to worldly standards;
  - to allow your flesh to control your desires.

→ To consider

- Consider where you might be over-indulging. The following list might help, although God may convict you of something that isn't on it: too much TV, sleep, food, alcohol; too much time at parties, the pub or the cinema; spending too much money on clothes or luxuries.

● If God speaks to you about something, work out exactly what you're going to do about it. Then do it.

Note: Overcoming temptation doesn't come naturally – you'll have to work at it. Pray daily that God will help you to resist and be strong.

The devil's . . . supreme object is to hurt Christ and Christ's cause. You personally are of no interest to him. It is only as you relate to Christ that you assume significance in his eyes . . . Do not flatter yourself. To God you are very important. But to Satan you are nothing more than a potentially useful microbe.

John White

24

Deliver Us from the Evil One

'But deliver us from the evil one.' (Matthew 6:13)

Put on the full armour of God so that you can take your
stand against the devil's schemes. (Ephesians 6:11)

People laugh at the devil (Satan), but the Bible takes him
seriously, describing him as a personal, spiritual being,
the source of evil and enemy of God. He tries to keep
unbelievers as far from God as possible, and he attacks
believers too. Jesus was on his hit list (Luke 4:1–12), and
if you're in Christ, so are you.

A clever enemy will keep his plans secret from the
opposing forces, and the devil will do his best to hide
his tactics from you. He knows where you're most
vulnerable, and will use your weaknesses to his advan-
tage. Of course, you're unlikely to see him, but you'll
hear his voice in your mind, or on the lips of others. If
you're not alert, you won't be able to stand against his
schemes.

Sometimes the devil will use subtle schemes. He'll
disguise himself as 'an angel of light' (2 Corinthians

11:14), and will try to deceive you. His suggestions will sound very reasonable, but they're actually designed to draw you away from God. The devil will often use people who are close to you to do this. Peter was one of Jesus' closest friends and wanted the best for him. But when he heard Jesus talking about his death, he rebuked him. The devil was behind Peter's words, and Jesus recognised this (Matthew 16:22–23).

The devil also uses the surprise attack. He will pounce on you like 'a roaring lion' (1 Peter 5:8) and will try to accuse or destroy you. He will roar out your faults, tell you that you're useless and claw at your faith in God. Satan tormented Paul, but Paul recognised his attacks and resisted him (2 Corinthians 12:7–10).

Our enemy is too subtle to use one tactic alone. He may come as an angel of light and a roaring lion, combining reasonable suggestions with personal accusations or disasters. We must 'be alert' (Ephesians 6:18). Soldiers who doze on the battlefield are asking for trouble.

We can't deliver ourselves from evil – Satan is too strong for us. But Jesus has defeated him on the cross, and if we're 'in Christ', his victory is ours. When the devil comes to us, we don't argue or fight with him. We submit to God and resist the devil, who must then flee from us (James 4:7). So when we pray, 'Deliver us from evil,' we're saying, 'Lord, I'm submitting my life to you. Help me to recognise and avoid the devil's schemes. If I resist him, I know that he has no choice but to leave me alone.'

⊡ Food for thought

The devil is evil.

- 'The serpent [devil] deceived me' (Genesis 3:13).
- '[The devil] was a murderer from the beginning, not holding to the truth, for there is no truth in him. When he lies, he speaks his native language, for he is a liar and the father of lies' (John 8:44).
- 'Satan . . . leads the whole world astray . . . the accuser of our brothers [Satan] . . . accuses them before our God day and night' (Revelation 12:9–10).

⊡ To discover

- Read Luke 4:1–12. How did Jesus defend himself against the devil's attacks (vv.4,8,12)?
- Read Ephesians 6:10–18. When you're tempted to get angry with people, what do you need to remember (v.12)?
- Go through the 'armour of God' and make sure that you understand it. If you don't, talk to a mature Christian.

⊡ To consider

- Pray through the earlier part of the Lord's Prayer and add, 'But deliver us from evil.'
- Pray that today God will help you to:
    - recognise the devil's tactics;
    - resist the devil.

- Read Deuteronomy 18:9–14.
- Have you been exposed to demonic activity (e.g. yoga, horoscopes, ouija boards, crystal gazing, etc.)? If so, follow these steps:
  - Repent: apologise to God and ask for his forgiveness.
  - Renounce: tell God you have left Satan's domain.
  - Destroy: destroy occult objects (charms, books, etc.).
  - Break: break contact with these activities.
  - Be filled: ask God to fill you with his Spirit.

  You might like to ask a mature Christian to pray with you about this.

The measure of our spirituality is the amount of praise and of thanksgiving in our prayers.

D. Martyn Lloyd-Jones

25

Kingdom, Power and Glory

'For yours is the kingdom and the power and the glory for ever. Amen.' (Matthew 6:13)

'Yours, O Lord, is the greatness and the power and the glory and the majesty and the splendour, for everything in heaven and on earth is yours. Yours, O Lord, is the kingdom; you are exalted as head over all.' (1 Chronicles 29:11–12)

Sometimes, when everything seems to be going wrong, you'll wonder if God is really in control – and if he is, why he doesn't do something.

Yes, God is in control. 'The Lord reigns,' says the psalmist (Psalm 99:1). And Jesus teaches us to pray to God, 'Yours is the kingdom.' Satan will try to mess things up, but he doesn't reign. Immediately God says to him, 'Enough!' he must back off.

When we pray, 'Yours is the kingdom,' we are declaring that God is King over everything – including our personal circumstances. We are praising him that he has brought us into his kingdom, and we are looking forward to our future in a kingdom in eternity.

The power also belongs to God. He made the earth by his power and rules by it too (Jeremiah 10:12; Psalm 66:7). You may get frustrated about your weakness and wonder how God can possibly use you, but God tells you that his 'power is made perfect in weakness' (2 Corinthians 12:9). You must learn to look at him and rely on his strength, not yours.

When we pray, 'Yours is the power,' we are reminding ourselves that without God we are weak. We are praising him for the power of the Holy Spirit and declaring that we will defeat the enemy through this power, and not through our own intellect or abilities. And we are remembering that one day his power will raise us up to be with him for ever (1 Corinthians 6:14).

God's glory shines through his character and the things he does. When Jesus came to earth, he revealed God's glory to us. He loved people and reached out to them. And now he wants you to do the same. As you let him change you, his glory will be reflected more and more in your life (2 Corinthians 3:18).

When we pray, 'Yours is the glory,' we are lifting up the name of God and declaring that he alone is worthy of all our praise. We are also thanking him that he's allowed us to share his glory while we're on earth. And we're looking forward to eternal glory in the future.

The Lord's Prayer ends by focusing our attention on God's greatness – inspiring us to finish our prayer time with praise. The kingdom, power and glory belong to God 'for ever and ever'. One day Jesus will return and we'll reign with him in heaven. Today we go out knowing that he is in charge, whatever happens.

➔ Food for thought

God's people will extol his greatness.

- 'All you have made will praise you, O Lord; your saints will extol you. They will tell of the glory of your kingdom and speak of your might, so that all men may know of your mighty acts and the glorious splendour of your kingdom. Your kingdom is an everlasting kingdom, and your dominion endures through all generations' (Psalm 145:10–13).

➔ To discover

- Read John 19:10–11. What did Pilate think he had? What did Jesus have to point out to him? Why doesn't God always exercise his power against evil?
- Over the next day or so memorise Romans 8:28. Whenever you face a difficult situation recite the verse to yourself.

➔ To consider

- Pray through the earlier part of the Lord's Prayer and add, 'For yours is the kingdom and the power and the glory for ever. Amen.'
- Praise God that he's brought you into his kingdom and affirm that he's King over your present situation.
- Thank God for the power of his Spirit and ask him to help you to live by his power today.

- Declare that God alone is worthy of praise and pray that he'll help you to live for his glory today.
- One day you will reign with Jesus in heaven. Worship God for this, and for being such a great King.

It will take violent dedication to prayer to bring the power of God into our lives. This violent earnestness will be most evident in discipline. For power in prayer takes much time. For this reason we must set priorities for our time. Many things will crowd around us to keep us from spending the time necessary for developing power in prayer.

Paul Y. Cho

26

Press On

One thing I do: Forgetting what is behind and straining towards what is ahead, I press on towards the goal to win the prize for which God has called me heavenwards in Christ Jesus. (Philippians 3:13–14)

It's easy to panic. You learn how to study the Bible and pray, and suddenly you wonder how you're going to keep it up. What happens if you're not getting anything out of the Bible? Will God be angry if you get halfway through the Lord's Prayer and then run out of time? Suddenly, spending time with Jesus sounds more like a burden than a joy.

What is happening here? You're thinking that if you fail you'll be letting God down. But that's not true. Jesus has fully satisfied God on your behalf. If you never open your Bible or pray again, he'll still love you as much at the end of your life as he does now. You don't read the Bible and pray to make God happy, but to know him better.

You'll find that you have to work hard at some passages of Scripture to get anything out of them. You'll get interrupted. You'll daydream in the middle of the Lord's

Prayer. And you may even fall asleep! It doesn't matter. God won't punish you by giving you an awful day! He'll just continue to love and bless you.

God wants to spend time with you. He wants to talk to you, answer your requests and use you to glorify his name. He invites you to enjoy an intimate relationship with him, but it won't come automatically. You'll need to discipline your life – not because you have to, but because you want to. You love God and can think of nothing better than spending time with him.

Discipline involves hard work. It's amazing what Olympic athletes can do. But what you see during the brief duration of the Olympics is the result of years of daily discipline in private. Your spiritual progress will be no different. Personal growth and public triumph will result from daily Bible reading and prayer in secret.

Some Christians set unrealistic prayer goals. They discover that others pray for two hours a day and they try to imitate them. But that's crazy. People who don't jog can't run a marathon, and God doesn't expect you to run a spiritual marathon before you've jogged a bit. So you start with thirty minutes a day and keep that up. Then you gradually build on this discipline.

If your plans don't begin with God, they'll be a burden to you. But if they are motivated by the Spirit, they will set you free.

⮕ Food for thought

God wants us to know him.

- 'Know that I am God' (Psalm 46:10).
- 'Let him who boasts boast about this: that he understands and knows me' (Jeremiah 9:24).
- 'This is eternal life: that they may know you, the only true God, and Jesus Christ, whom you have sent' (John 17:3).
- 'I consider everything a loss compared to the surpassing greatness of knowing Christ Jesus my Lord' (Philippians 3:8).

➔ To discover

- Read 1 Corinthians 9:24–27. In your notebook write down what God is saying to you through these verses. Write down how you're going to respond to him.
- Start a prayer diary. Write down the date and your main prayer requests, and leave space to add God's answer, and the date when he replies. Don't use this book for every prayer request – just for the main ones. You may only refer to it once a month. It should encourage you.

➔ To consider

- It's a good idea to have a prayer partner – someone you can talk to and pray with on a regular basis. This person could be your husband or wife (if he or she is a Christian). It could be someone else of the same sex as you. Why not ask someone to be your prayer partner?

As the Lord of history, God is controlling all of its events, not only on earth but in all realms, to serve His purpose of bringing to maturity and eventually to enthronement with His Son, not angels or archangels, but the Church, His chosen Bride.

Paul E. Billheimer

27

To the Ends of the Earth

All the ends of the earth will see the salvation of our God.
(Isaiah 52:10)

People who know exactly what they want to do are really inspiring. Somehow you sense they are going to succeed whatever it costs them.

God has always had a definite goal: to win a people for his Son from all the nations of the world. That people he calls the church. Way back in Genesis he promised to bless Abraham and all the nations through him. And later he told Jesus that he would use him to 'bring my salvation to the ends of the earth' (Isaiah 49:6). Jesus knew that he wasn't on this planet merely to reach out to a few individuals. He was here to win the world – whatever it cost him.

Jesus wanted his disciples to catch this vision. 'You will receive power when the Holy Spirit comes on you; and you will be my witnesses . . . to the ends of the earth,' he told them (Acts 1:8). They knew from the start that they needed the Holy Spirit's power to tell others about Jesus. They also knew that their mission was meant to go much further than their own backyard in Jerusalem.

Once they had received the Spirit at Pentecost, there was no stopping them. Burning in their hearts was a passion to reach the nations for Jesus. So they preached the gospel everywhere, and within twenty years they had touched the known world of their day.

It is easy to miss God's goal. When you are born again, everything is new and exciting. God is changing and blessing you. And maybe he's doing some great things in the local church too. It is tempting to forget that there is a world out there that God wants you to reach.

When God told Abraham, 'I will bless you,' Abraham could have become self-centred. He could have thought, 'God's favour rests on me. Isn't that nice!' But God made sure that he understood that the blessing wasn't for him alone. It was for 'all peoples on earth' (Genesis 12:3). Abraham had to get the right perspective from the start; so did the disciples; so must we.

The last words that Jesus said before he returned to heaven were, '. . . to the ends of the earth.' They must have rung in the disciples' ears as they made their way back to Jerusalem. What words ring in your ears? Do you hear God saying to you, 'You're just an individual I'm blessing in this little corner'? Or do you hear him declaring to you, 'I'm after a people for my Son. You're part of a great army that I'm raising up and mobilising to reach the world'?

➔ Food for thought

Our mission is to the whole world.

- 'And this gospel of the kingdom will be preached in the whole world as a testimony to all nations, and then the end will come' (Matthew 24:14).
- 'Go and make disciples of all nations' (Matthew 28:18).
- 'Go into all the world and preach the good news to all creation' (Mark 16:15).
- 'For God so loved the world that he gave his one and only Son' (John 3:16).

→ To discover

- Read Matthew 24:14. What must happen before the end of the world comes?
- One day Jesus and the church will be united. The Bible says that it will be like a wedding between a bridegroom and his bride. Read about this in Revelation 19:6–9.
- The bride (church) will be made up of Christians from every people group on earth. Read about this in Revelation 5:9–10 and Revelation 7:9–10. (*Note*: the 'Lamb' is Jesus.)
- Every Christian is part of Christ's bride. Write down in your notebook how you think Jesus would like his bride to be (e.g. faithful, not a gossip, friendly, etc.). Are you like this?

→ To consider

- Read Genesis 12:2–3. Ask God to show you how you can be more involved in reaching the world. His answer may not be something dramatic like:

'Go to India.' He is more likely to tell you to pray for other countries, or to give money to a Christian who is on the mission field. He may encourage you to begin a prayer group for a certain place in the world, or to speak about him to your neighbours.

- Keep God's goal in your heart. One day he may call you to go somewhere else to tell people about him.

We have a story to tell the nations, but it is also a story to tell to the neighbours.

Vance Havner

28

You Will Be My Witnesses

Jesus . . . said, 'Go home to your family and tell them how much the Lord has done for you, and how he has had mercy on you.' So the man went away and began to tell in the Decapolis how much Jesus had done for him. And all the people were amazed. (Mark 5:19–20)

When Jesus set a man free from evil spirits that man was so grateful that he went off and told everyone what Jesus had done for him. And the people were amazed.

That is what it means to be a witness. You understand what Jesus has done for you and you can't keep quiet. No one is forcing you to speak – you want to. You are so grateful to Jesus that you can't help it. People may ignore you, or laugh at you and say you're just going through a phase. But they can't deny the reality of what you have. That will amaze them.

Jesus has given you his power to witness, and he wants you to rely on that power and not on your own strength. You may get your words muddled and your theology wrong. You may get stuck when people ask questions. Don't worry. Jesus doesn't expect you to know it all. Just say what he has done and let his Spirit use you.

Witnessing must be motivated by love. Zealous Christians sometimes forget this. You can't fault their keenness, but you cringe at their methods. Some of them preach judgement and hellfire, while others try to argue individuals into the kingdom. But the goal is to win people for Jesus, not to put them off.

Jesus was a 'friend of . . . sinners' (Matthew 11:19). He accepted people as they were and took an interest in them. When people see you as their friend, they'll listen to you. So if you're chatting to someone at the bus stop, relate to him. Talk about ordinary things: the weather, holidays, the music scene. . . Don't pry, just be friendly. When you know the person feels accepted, you can say, 'I thought I was doing OK, but I've since found something better – a real peace and purpose in life. Can I tell you about it?'

Witnessing is about actions as well as words. Usually, people who are close to you will be more impressed by what you do than what you say. So once they know what has happened to you, don't keep badgering them. Just live out your new life. Be kind and helpful – to them and to others. Pray for them and speak when Jesus gives you the opportunity.

If people aren't interested in Jesus, don't argue with them or become discouraged. Be polite and let them believe what they want to. They may ask you questions later. Concentrate on speaking to people who want to listen to you. God will honour you, and one day he'll give you the joy of leading someone to Christ.

➔ Food for thought

We must watch how we speak.

- 'Words from a wise man's mouth are gracious' (Ecclesiastes 10:12).
- 'All . . . were amazed at the gracious words that came from [Jesus'] lips' (Luke 4:22).
- 'Do not let any unwholesome talk come out of your mouths, but only what is helpful for building others up according to their needs' (Ephesians 4:29).
- 'Let your conversation be always full of grace, seasoned with salt' (Colossians 4:6).

➔ To discover

- Underline these verses in your Bible. Write them down on a piece of paper and keep it in the cover.
  - The problem: sin separates (Isaiah 53:6; 59:2).
  - Sin's penalty (Romans 3:23; 6:23).
  - God's answer: Jesus died for us (1 Peter 2:24; 3:18).
  - Our response: repent (Acts 2:38; 3:19).
  - Believe and receive (John 1:12; 3:16).

  Use these verses when someone asks you how they can become a Christian. (*Note*: Make sure you understand them first.)
- A personal testimony will come across with greater impact if you know it well. Write down the following headings and work out what you can say under each:

- Where I was.
- What the central focus of my life was before I was saved (e.g. drugs, loneliness, desire for money, etc.).
- What happened.
- Why I decided to become a Christian.
- Where I am now.
- The most important things Jesus has done for me.

- Practise your testimony with a friend until you can present it naturally and clearly in about three minutes.

➔ To consider

- Write down the names of any colleagues or friends who don't know you are a Christian.
- Pray for opportunities to tell them about Jesus.

I've seen Jesus perform all the healing miracles that He did in the Gospels. He's using me in this ministry, but I long to see signs and wonders multiplied throughout the church.

Mahesh Chavda

29

Signs and Wonders

'The Spirit of the Lord is on me, because he has anointed me to preach good news to the poor. He has sent me to proclaim freedom for the prisoners and recovery of sight for the blind, to release the oppressed, to proclaim the year of the Lord's favour.' (Luke 4:18–19)

Jesus told his disciples, 'As the Father has sent me, I am sending you' (John 20:21). So how was Jesus sent? Did God say, 'I just want you to preach the gospel and bring people into the kingdom'? No. Jesus' mission was far more dynamic than that. He was sent to preach, heal and deliver. His words were accompanied by signs and wonders.

What Jesus began, he wanted his disciples to continue. He sent out the Twelve with the command to 'preach the kingdom of God and to heal the sick' (Luke 9:2), which is exactly what they did. Then he gave the same commission to seventy-two others (Luke 10:9), and they fulfilled it too. When Jesus returned to heaven, the Christians in the early church continued his preaching, healing and deliverance ministry, because that is what he had sent them to do.

Jesus never said, 'The miracles will fizzle out once the church gets established.' Nor did he say, 'Miracles should be done only by respected church leaders.' What he actually said was, 'Preach the good news to all creation . . . And these signs will accompany those who believe' (Mark 16:15,17). If you're a believer, Jesus has sent you to tell others about him and to perform the signs that will prove to people that the kingdom of God has come.

Some Christians are called to a ministry of signs and wonders. You may be one of them, you may not. God will reveal this to you in his time. What he wants you to do now is reach out to others whenever you get the opportunity.

Don't be frightened to move out in faith. Be excited. You may not be able to heal a blind person, but why not pray for a friend or a neighbour who has a cold? Of course, you'll need to be sensitive. Do they want you to pray for them? Do they mind if you put a hand on their shoulder? If you are not the same sex as the other person, it might be wise to take with you a Christian who is. You know the situation – you decide.

God may heal the person, but if he doesn't, don't be discouraged. What have you lost? You've asked God to bless someone. He or she is probably amazed that you care so much about them, and may be willing to hear more about Jesus later. Besides, you can't predict how God will answer. Some healing is gradual. You just keep reaching out and leaving the outcome in God's hands – it's what you've been sent to do.

⮕ Food for thought

Signs should accompany preaching.

- 'Now, Lord . . . enable your servants to speak your word with great boldness. Stretch out your hand to heal and perform miraculous signs and wonders through the name of your holy servant Jesus' (Acts 4:29–30).
- 'Our gospel came to you not simply with words, but also with power, with the Holy Spirit and deep conviction' (1 Thessalonians 1:5).

⮕ To discover

- Read John 12:12–14. In your notebook write down the answers to the following questions:
  - Why do you think Jesus said, 'I tell you the truth,' here?
  - Who can do what he did?
  - What do you think it means to 'ask in Jesus' name'?
  - What's the goal of answered prayer?
  - Do you believe what Jesus said?
- Read Matthew 17:14–21. Success doesn't depend on you, but on your faith. Keep praying for faith and take every opportunity to put it into action. The more you see God's power at work, the more your faith will grow.

→ To consider

- When we reach out to people, we shouldn't rely on our own ability but on the power of the Holy Spirit.
- There's only one 'baptism in the Spirit', but we can receive fresh fillings of the Spirit (see Acts 4:31). Ask God to give you a fresh filling of the Holy Spirit today.
- Begin to reach out in faith and pray for healing. Expect God to work.

[A brother in China] stood up in the meeting and began to share about what had happened in prison. Everyone began to weep and I at first thought they felt bad for the suffering he had to endure. Then I heard people saying, 'Lord, how blessed he is that he can suffer for You. Oh, that You would allow me the same privilege.' I realised they were all envious of this brother for he was especially chosen of the Lord for this honour.

Dennis Balcombe

30

Persecution

In fact, everyone who wants to live a godly life in Christ
Jesus will be persecuted. (2 Timothy 3:12)

If you are insulted because of the name of Christ, you are
blessed, for the Spirit of glory and of God rests on you.
(1 Peter 4:14)

You can't get away from it. If you want to follow Jesus
with all your heart, you'll be persecuted. Lots of
Christians have discovered this. Some have had to face
mockery, torture and even death for what they believed.

Maybe you have already faced persecution. You
really want your family or friends to receive Christ
themselves, so you tell them what he's done for you. But
instead of accepting what you say, they reject it and
ridicule your faith in God. It is hard to cope with that,
but at the same time it should encourage you. It is a
clear sign that you belong to Jesus. Let's look at three
guidelines on persecution.

First, try to avoid it. Some Christians get a persecution
complex. They almost want to be persecuted because it

somehow looks good to be a martyr. But that's the wrong attitude. God won't bless us if we're trying to be great – only if we're faithfully following him. So do all you can to avoid persecution, but if it does come, welcome it. God's glory rests on you if you're insulted for Jesus' sake (1 Peter 4:14).

Second, God will always give you enough grace for the test. As you go on in the Christian life, you'll find that some trials are more intense than others. When the trial is quite small, God will give you sufficient grace for it. When it's bigger, he will increase his grace. You may think, 'I couldn't go through torture for Christ.' But if God has that in mind for you, he'll give you grace for it when you need it, not now.

Third, people hate God, not you. Christians can't be proud of being persecuted, because persecution isn't really being directed at them. It's directed at Christ. People don't hate you, or your morality. They hate Jesus' righteousness in you. They can't understand your obedience. Christ in you challenges them and makes them afraid, so they lash out at you.

Unbelievers live for now. They think that this world is all there is, and they're satisfied if they can get what they want out of it. Christians are different. By faith they can see something that unbelievers can't – a heavenly city – and it excites them and motivates all they do.

If you're looking for an earthly reward, you'll come unstuck when you face persecution for Christ. But if you're gripped by the vision of a reward in heaven, you'll be able to face all opposition on earth. You'll go through anything to see the name of Jesus exalted in your life.

⤷ Food for thought

Christians will suffer.

- 'If we are children, then we are heirs – heirs of God and co-heirs with Christ, if indeed we share in his sufferings in order that we may also share in his glory' (Romans 8:17).
- 'It has been granted to you on behalf of Christ not only to believe on him, but also to suffer for him' (Philippians 1:29).
- 'If you suffer as a Christian, do not be ashamed, but praise God that you bear that name' (1 Peter 4:16).

⤷ To discover

- Read 1 Peter 3:13–18. In your notebook write down the answers to the following questions:
  - If you suffer for doing right, are you blessed even if you don't feel blessed?
  - How do you think you set apart Christ as Lord?
  - What should you do whenever people ask you about your faith in Jesus?
  - How should you do this?
  - With what result?
- Read John 15:18–21. Why does the world hate you?
- Read Luke 6:22–23. How does Jesus want you to respond to persecution?

⮕ To consider

- Read James 1:12 and 1 Corinthians 9:25. Are you seeking a 'crown' in heaven, or a reward on earth?
- Read Matthew 5:11–12. Why are you to rejoice?

Brothers, this Lord Jesus
Shall return again
With His Father's glory,
With His angel train;
For all wreaths of empire
Meet upon His brow,
And our hearts confess Him
King of glory now.

Caroline M. Noel

31

The End

'This same Jesus, who has been taken from you into heaven, will come back in the same way you have seen him go into heaven.' (Acts 1:11)

Jesus is coming back! One day everyone will see him come down from heaven. Then those who died believing will rise to meet him, and we – if we're Christians – will join them in the clouds. From that time on, we'll be with Jesus for ever.

Unbelievers are afraid of what happens after death. But Christians should be excited about it. The Bible doesn't just tell us that we're going to heaven, it says that God 'made us for this very purpose' (2 Corinthians 5:4–5). Death is God's ultimate plan for every believer.

Some Christians don't realise this. They think that if they are not careful they might not finish what God has given them to do. So they live rather cautiously. Paul didn't do that. He was in constant danger. He was beaten, imprisoned and shipwrecked. He wanted to do everything that God had planned for him, but he didn't see death as a tragic loss. For him it was glorious gain.

We tend to cling to our bodies, but Paul 'groaned' to leave his (Romans 8:23) and actually said that he would prefer to be with Christ (Philippians 1:23). So why was he so keen to die? Because God had shown him paradise (2 Corinthians 12:1–4). That magnificent vision was enough to dispel any fears that he had about dying. He knew what was coming, and it really excited him.

This life is a mist compared with what is to come. God wants Christians to enjoy life, but he knows that it will always be unsatisfying. So he encourages us to look beyond it to a day when everything will be perfect, when we'll have new bodies to replace our old worn-out ones, and when we'll be like Jesus and reign with him in heaven (Revelation 22:5).

It's so easy to think that one day death will come and pounce on us. But Paul never taught us that life would be swallowed up by death. Instead he said that 'what is mortal will be swallowed up by life' (2 Corinthians 5:4). Jesus has 'abolished death' (2 Timothy 2:10). It's not death that is pursuing the believer. It's life!

For a Christian, dying is the fulfilment of God's purpose. It is the gateway to a glorious inheritance. It is about going home to be with God for ever. Let these truths motivate and excite you! Say to God, 'I'm not going to live for this present world. I'm going to serve you in the light of eternity.' You'll find real freedom when you do that.

➔ Food for thought

We must aim for a reward in heaven.

- 'We make it our goal to please him . . . For we must all appear before the judgment seat of Christ, that each one may receive what is due to him for the things done while in the body, whether good or bad' (2 Corinthians 5:9–10).

- '[Moses] regarded disgrace for the sake of Christ as of greater value than the treasures of Egypt, because he was looking ahead to his reward' (Hebrews 11:26).

→ To discover

- Read Matthew 24:36,42–44. When will Jesus return? What two things must we do (vv.42,44)?
- Read 1 Corinthians 15:35–58. Write down in your notebook what will happen to you at the resurrection of the dead (i.e. God will give me a new imperishable body; this body will be glorious . . .).
- In the light of what's going to happen, how should we live (v.58)?
- Read Philippians 3:12–21. Jesus gave Paul a task to take hold of:
  - Where was his mind focused – on heavenly or earthly things?
  - Where are the minds of unbelievers focused?
  - Where is the believer's citizenship – in heaven or on earth?

→ To consider

- Read 1 Thessalonians 5:13–18.

- If you have any fears about death, pray about these and ask God why you have them. You might find it helpful to ask another Christian to pray with you about this.

Bibliography

The quotations in the studies are all used by permission.

1. J. John, *A New Creation* (Nelson Word Ltd, 1993).
2. Margaret Ellis, *Caring for New Christians* (Nelson Word Ltd, 1993).
3. David Watson, *Discipleship* (Hodder & Stoughton, 1981).
4. W. E. Vine, *Expository Dictionary of Bible Words* (Marshall Morgan & Scott, 1981).
5. Terry Virgo, *Restoration in the Church* (Kingsway Publications, 1985).
6. Colin Urquhart, *Anything You Ask* (Hodder & Stoughton, 1978).
7. Stephen Gaukroger, *Making it Work* (Scripture Union, 1990).
8. Charles Stanley, *The Wonderful Spirit Filled Life* (Nelson Word Ltd, 1992).
9. Donald S. Whitney, *Spiritual Disciplines for the Christian Life* (Scripture Press Foundation (UK) Ltd, 1991).

10. Charles Colson, *Faith on the Line* (Scripture Press Foundation (UK) Ltd, 1994).
11. David Watson, *I Believe in the Church* (Hodder & Stoughton, 1978).
12. *People of Destiny* magazine, March/April 1994.
13. Woodrow Knoll, *10 First Steps for the New Christian* (The Good News Broadcasting Association, Inc. Back to the Bible, 1992).
14. A. W. Tozer, *Of God and Men* (Christian Publications).
15. Larry Lea, *Learning the Joy of Prayer* (Kingsway Publications, 1989).
16. Richard J. Foster, *Prayer* (Hodder & Stoughton, 1992).
17. David Watson, *Discipleship* (Hodder & Stoughton, 1981).
18. Paul Y. Cho, *Praying with Jesus* (Nelson Word Ltd, 1987).
19. Arthur Wallis, *Going on God's Way* (Kingsway Publications, 1987).
20. Paul Y. Cho, *Praying with Jesus* (Nelson Word Ltd, 1987).
21. John White, *People in Prayer* (InterVarsity Christian Fellowship, USA, 1977).
22. David Augsburger, *Caring Enough to Forgive* (Regal Books, USA, 1981).
23. *Daily Readings from the Works of Martyn Lloyd-Jones* selected by Frank Cumbers (Methodist Publishing House, 1970).
24. John White, *The Fight* (InterVarsity Christian Fellowship, USA, 1991).
25. D. Martyn Lloyd-Jones, *Studies in the Sermon on*

the Mount (InterVarsity Press, 1976).

26. Paul Y. Cho with R. Whitney Manzano, *Prayer: Key to Revival* (Nelson Word Ltd, 1984).

27. Paul E. Billheimer, *Destined for the Throne* (Christian Literature Crusade, Inc., 1975).

28. Woodrow Knoll, *10 First Steps for the New Christian* (The Good News Broadcasting Association, Inc. Back to the Bible, 1992).

29. Mahesh Chavda, *God's Miraculous Power*, Oasis Series (Frontier Publishing International, Nelson Word Ltd, 1993).

30. *Hong Kong & China Report*.

31. Bruce Milne, *The End of the World* (Kingsway Publications Ltd, 1979).